The Traditions of
Christmas

The Traditions of
Christmas

The Editors of Victoria *Magazine*

HEARST BOOKS
A Division of Sterling Publishing Co., Inc.
NEW YORK

Copyright © 1992 by Hearst Communications, Inc.

Copyright notices, permissions, and acknowledgments appear on page 144.

This book was previously published as a hardcover and as a paperback under the title *Victoria The Heart of Christmas*.

Produced by Smallwood & Stewart Inc., New York City
Edited by Laurie Orseck
Interior design by Barbara Scott-Goodman
Text by Mary Goodbody, Catherine Revland, Arlene Stewart, and Linda Sunshine

Library of Congress Cataloging-in-Publication Data
Available upon request.

10   9   8   7   6   5   4   3   2   1

Published by Hearst Books
A Division of Sterling Publishing Co., Inc.
387 Park Avenue South, New York, NY 10016

Victoria is a trademark owned by Hearst Magazines Property, Inc., in USA,
and Hearst Communications, Inc., in Canada.
Hearst Books is a trademark of Hearst Communications, Inc.

www.victoriamag.com

Distributed in Canada by Sterling Publishing
c/o Canadian Manda Group, One Atlantic Avenue, Suite 105
Toronto, Ontario, Canada M6K 3E7

Distributed in Australia by Capricorn Link (Australia) Pty. Ltd.
P.O. Box 704, Windsor, NSW 2756 Australia

NOTICE: Every effort has been made to locate the copyright owners of the material used in this book.
Please let us know if an error has been made, and we will make any necessary changes in subsequent printings.

Printed in Singapore

ISBN 1-58816-293-1

Contents

Foreword
11

FOREWORD

For a *Victoria* Christmas, we stretch out our arms and gather in all the wonderment that abounds in this season of joy. And how fortunate we are that so many people all over the world respond to this holiday in the spirit of Dickens, blessing everyone.

The pages of this book are a special expression of the *Victoria* Christmas tradition. When all the plays and pageants have been performed, when all the trees have been trimmed with ornaments that hold the memories of Christmases past, when all the beautifully wrapped gifts have been opened, we arrive at the Christmas of the heart, of love and understanding. It is with hearts open that we come to tables laden with delicacies, and it is with hearts overflowing that we celebrate this season, bringing friends and family together with a glow as warm as candlelight.

There is no season of the year that delights us as much as Christmastime. Surely no period allows us to revel in our nineteenth-century heritage as does this one; Christmas as we celebrate it today is full of Victorian resonance, from the carols we sing to the trees we trim. And so it is with great pride that we bring you *The Traditions of Christmas*, with our heartfelt wish that your own holidays will be richer because of the ideas and inspiration assembled here. More than anything, we hope you will find as much joy as we have had in creating these pages. From our *Victoria* family to yours, the happiest of holidays—filled, most of all, with love.

—The Editors of *Victoria* Magazine

CHAPTER ONE

The Homecoming

Tomorrow comes December

And winterfalls of old

Are with me from the past

A. E. Housman
Eight O'Clock

December. Wrapped in warm woolens,

we share a sleigh ride with

friends, or just enjoy the beauty of the

snow. By afternoon,

when the sun is on

the wane, comes the

invigorating sound of boots stamping off snow

on the porch steps and a chorus of voices

welcoming us in to sit by a

blazing fire, reunited with

family once more. In this

world of opposites, the cold and dark against the

warm and gay, the pleasures of Christmastime are

all the more keenly felt: the

colors richer, the music sweeter,

the food a regal feast.

The Christmas of our fondest dreams is the snowy homecoming, the family reunion, the comforting warmth of our childhood home.

The gathering always takes place at the roomiest house, where baking and household preparations have been going on for weeks. In many families the rule of "every available relative" that Charles Dickens wrote of in *Great Expectations* still applies. By plane, by car, and from down the street the cast of characters arrives — brothers and sisters, children, aunts and uncles and cousins, grandparents, old chums and new friends.

The familiarity of Christmas is perhaps its greatest charm—the assurance that this year will be like the last, that the repetition of small rituals can always be counted on: the tree that is chosen and trimmed according to a time-honored text; the pleas by the host and hostess to eat more; the children's homemade gifts, wrapped with such care and delivered with such solemnity; the collection of ornaments that grows by half a box each year, every one with its own story to tell.

Every year there is the one gift that must be tracked

down from store to store, and one carton of decorations that gets lost in the frenzy. Every year the kitchen is the scene of a vast orchestration, exquisitely timed, to produce a feast, lovingly prepared from recipes that have been in the family for generations. And at the table, covered with a snow-white cloth, with candles gleaming and crystal sparkling, an extraordinary thing happens: The commingling of familiar voices becomes like a carol, remembering and retelling the precious memories of family history—the gift of the hand-knitted sweater with just one sleeve; the year the tree fell over; the Christmas Eve snowstorm spent in terminals and along the highway, followed by a joyful day of feasting when everyone finally arrived.

In every family a set of Christmas traditions grows over time, in which the years are marked and small joys take on a special private meaning. Time adds layer upon layer of meaning, and the Christmas spirit is coaxed along until it envelops the house in its wondrous warmth. The great charm of the season is that it is not a particular place or time but a spirit of warmth, generosity, and good will that is always welcome everywhere.

This grand 1860's Italianate villa in northwestern Connecticut (opposite) has been restored to its former grace and beauty by its present owners—a labor of love carried out almost solely with their own hands. A reminder of the houses built in an age of large families, it has been the setting for holiday celebrations for several genera-tions. 🕊 *Delicate white lilies grace an elegant front-door wreath (above). The flowers, kept fresh in florists' vials, are tucked into a simple wreath of juniper boughs, thick with their seasonal frosty blue berries, and tied with a silken ribbon. These fresh flowers will withstand near-freezing temperatures, despite their fragile nature.*

The sight of gleaming white country church spires reaching up into the juniper blue of a winter sky is one that can send many a lagging Christmas spirit soaring. Although a country Christmas, like a snowy one, is only a fantasy for many of us, rural churches

with their architectural grace lie deep at the heart of Christmas custom, and are a reminder that long ago the season was celebrated communally rather than at home. It was in them that all of life's most important passages were marked, in them that the secular and sacred needs of the community were met.

On Christmas Eve, the churches were filled with people from altar to vestibule, the air steaming from snowy coats warming to a slow crescendo of heat and light, increasing as each arrival lit a candle and the sexton solemnly attended to the hundreds of tiny flames on the massive fresh-cut tree. When the candle lighting was completed—the sexton standing by with a pail of water, pole, and sponge, "just in case"—the children came up one by one to receive a gift and a bag of nuts, fruit, and candy.

Then finally, throats fired up by melting peppermint, the community sang the traditional carols and expressed their yearning for peace. The music was sung in four-part harmony, and although the congregation was led by a choir, everyone knew every verse by heart. The same carols are sung today, the oldest of which date back to the twelfth century. They are as unchanging a part of Christmas as the bringing in of greens and the spirit of gift giving.

These churches are still the center of community life, and never more so than during this holiday. The countryside reverberates on Christmas morning, with bells tolling and chiming from the steeples of all the little churches that dot the landscape. In the cold and crystalline air of late December bell sounds travel far, and the pealing blends into a chorus with many melodies. Legend has it that the clappers of bells are really the tongues of angels, and that their ringing casts out evil spirits. The church bells seem to create a spell, and their chimes like a greeting through the air:

> "Ring in the nobler modes of life
> With sweeter manner, purer laws
> The larger heart, the kindlier hand . . . "

The sentiments of the Victorian poet Alfred, Lord Tennyson remain strong in us today. The great enduring mystery of Christmas is how it can warm even the most unlikely heart, and how each year it moves our souls to acknowledge the power of generosity and the depth of our yearnings for peace.

18

In the small Connecticut towns of Cornwall and Washington (above and opposite), these Gothic-style churches, elegant in their whitewashed simplicity, mark the Christmas season by the tolling of their steeple bells. ❧ The beautiful stone angel in the courtyard of St. Bridget's Church in Cornwall (above right) is a silent reminder that angels were once believed to communicate with mortals through the sound of pealing bells. ❧ The resplendent holly red doors of St. Bridget's (right) are a wonderful backdrop for a pair of welcoming holiday wreaths that have been studded with natural offerings: pine cones, rose hips, and silvery sage.

*E*very Christmas should begin with the sound of bells, and when I was a child mine always did. But they were sleigh bells, not church bells, for we lived in a part of Cedar Rapids, Iowa, where there were no churches. My bells were on my father's team of horses as he drove up to our horse-headed hitching post with the bobsled that would take us to celebrate Christmas on the family farm ten miles out in the country. My father would bring the team down Fifth Avenue at a small trot, flicking his whip over the horses' rump and making the bells double their light, thin jangling over the snow, whose radiance threw back a brilliance like the sound of bells . . .

There are no such departures any more: the whole family piling into the bobsled with a foot of golden oat straw to lie in and heavy buffalo robes to lie under, the horses stamping the soft snow, and at every motion of their hoofs the bells jingling, jingling.

There are no streets like those any more: the snow sensibly left on the road for the sake of sleighs and easy travel. We could hop off and ride the heavy runners as they made their hissing, tearing sound over the packed snow. And along the streets we met other horses, so that we moved from one set of bells to another, from the tiny tinkle of the individual bells on the shafts to the silvery, leaping sound of the long strands hung over the harness.

There are no such arrivals any more: the harness bells ringing and clashing, the horses whinny- ing at the horses in the barn and receiving a great, trumpeting whinny in reply, the dogs leaping into the bobsled and burrowing under the buffalo robes, a squawking from the hen house, a yelling of "Whoa, whoa," at the excited horses, boy and girl cousins howling around the bobsled, and the descent into the snow with the Christmas basket carried by my mother.

Paul Engle
An Iowa Christmas

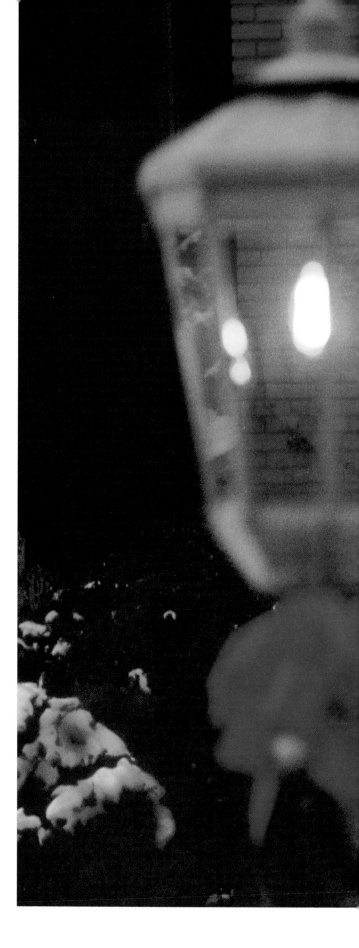

$\mathcal{A}$lthough the lights of the city are never more resplendent than at Christmas, the ones at home seem to burn the brightest, and a tree in the window glimmers like a beacon that draws us home, to eat well and often, to linger at night by the fire until long past bedtime, to share the latest tales and reminisce about the best of times. Home is the soul of Christmas, and the tree its centerpiece, drawing the eye to contemplate the wonders within. ❧ When the gentry of Louisville, Kentucky, built their mansions during the Gilded Age, they turned the area around St. James Court into a neighborhood that one London observer called "more English than the English" (right). Cast-iron gas lamps from the 1890's still weave their spell on the street where lavish holiday decorations grace every house. ❧ Electric candles flickering behind heirloom lace curtains (above) enchant passersby.

CHAPTER TWO

The Children's Holiday

I danced in the morning

When the world was begun

And I danced in the moon

And the stars and the sun . . .

Sydney Carter
Lord of the Dance

Is it possible to think of Christmas

without thinking of children?

They are central to the magic, and from

the choirboy and bell ringer to the littlest

Nutcracker angel, they are the stars of the

holiday season's

special pageantry.

Christmas is a time

to reaffirm the need to

believe, and children make

it possible for us to sustain

hope and faith.

It is through their delight and wonder that

we are able to

truly appreciate the

joys of the season.

On a crisp, snowy day, a young child stands perfectly still, oblivious to the cold, transfixed by the scenes in a magnificent store window. She is visiting Lord & Taylor, the oldest department store in New York City, where each year exacting miniature scenes from a Christmas past are created in their Fifth Avenue windows. Beyond the glass, adults going about their business and children at their play a hundred years ago are caught in mid-motion: Busy Christmas shoppers hail a carriage, a horse eats from his feed bag, and skaters warm themselves at an outdoor fire. This is an animated place, where little dogs wag their tails and skaters fall. Children love the idea of a Lilliputian world where adults are just slightly larger than dolls. Adults are fascinated by the re-creation of history, studying every detail of the costumes and the settings.

These fantastic window displays are the result of long and careful planning. Richard Pollard and his design staff begin creating the dioramas each year in March. For these windows, the research involved a visit to Washington Irving's house, Sunnyside, which is now a museum; the fairy-tale quality the designers found there lent itself beau-

tifully to the creation of the Hudson River series. Back in the studio, work goes on at a brisk pace right up until the windows are installed, just before Thanksgiving. "The idea of replicating the past in miniature as accurately as possible intrigues people," the designer says. "The result is a three-dimensional look at what life might have really looked like in those times."

Minute attention is paid to every detail, down to the lintels and the lapels, and the gorgeous nineteenth-century attire is made with special meticulousness, using miniature ironing boards and even smaller irons. Pollard and his staff are always on the lookout for materials to carry out their designs. For instance, the snow that seems to turn so deliciously into icicles on the roofs of the hansom cabs is crafted of ground crystals of coarse salt. Round cosmetic bulbs provide perfect gaslight shades, and toothpaste caps are ideal as furniture legs. Fabric patterns must be small enough in scale so they don't overpower the mannequins: Even the burliest figure is less than twenty inches tall.

Each year the crowds' response is rich reward for Richard Pollard. "It's magical," he says. "People say they wish they could crawl right into the scenes."

A *young girl gazes at the replica of turn-of-the-century Grand Central Station, elegantly garlanded for Christmas (opposite), in windows tracing a trip up New York's Hudson River.* *The last stop is the Grand Union Hotel in Saratoga Springs (top left), duplicated down to the smallest detail.* *Father Christmas (top right) appears as he was depicted in the nineteenth century, with a long red velvet cloak and hood.* *Landscape painter Frederick Church (above left), of the Hudson River School, is shown at his easel near his mansion, Olana.* *A well-dressed shopper (above right) owes her winter attire to strips of plaid ribbon.*

The centerpiece of one of the Lord & Taylor windows is Sunnyside, Washington Irving's house in Tarrytown, New York, which has changed very little since the author and his sisters lived there. "The house is a quaint combination of Dutch Colonial and Gothic revival," recalls designer Richard Pollard, "which lent itself well to a Christmas setting." Using a portrait of the author as his guide, Pollard depicted Irving greeting his guests on a Christmas Eve just before the Civil War. The lamp bearer, dressed in medieval clothing, represents the way Christmas was celebrated before Queen Victoria's time, with medieval mummeries and mystery plays.

Nutcracker smiled down at her. "There are many things you've never seen that I should like to show you."

And he led her up the ladder and into the land of toys.

Snow was falling thickly, but it was not the least cold. When Marie caught a snowflake on her tongue, she was astounded to discover that it tasted just like sugar. Up ahead stood a pine forest that glittered and sparkled with gold and silver fruit and gave off the most delicious fragrance of orange and spices.

"This is Christmas Wood," said Nutcracker.

He clapped his hands and instantly there appeared a group of little shepherds and shepherdesses, so white and delicate that you would have thought they were made of sugar. Other little figures with reed flutes and pipes appeared from behind the trees; and as they played their sweet music, the shepherds and shepherdesses danced for Marie.

E.T.A. Hoffman, adapted by Janet Schulman
The Nutcracker

Far from the excitement of the city, in the highlands of New England where the family of Tasha Tudor has lived since the seventeenth century, the beloved children's book writer lovingly assembles an old-fashioned homemade country Christmas for her children and grandchildren each year. The author freely admits her preference for the past and has even created an entire "family" of dolls to live in that gentler world, including Emma, her alter ego and favorite character.

Crossing the threshold of Tasha's Vermont farmhouse is also a journey into the past, for the author shuns electricity and other modern conveniences save the telephone. The first room is the winter kitchen, that central room of many old farmhouses where the family gathered by the warmth of an enormous hearth and oven. Here the stage is set for the high drama that is a Tasha Tudor Christmas.

"It all begins long before December," she says. "In fact, we think of Christmas all year round. When I was a child it seemed an eternity from Christmas to Christmas, but now it seems like no time at all." The process begins in earnest at harvest time, when the best of the pears are bottled for gifts, and the sweetest raspberry preserves are put up. As the nights lengthen, the activity indoors gathers momentum. The author spends many hours knitting mittens and socks, drawing pictures, and making dolls and other presents. When each gift is finished, it is added to the items already set aside in a massive leather trunk known as the Christmas chest. In November, beeswax candle ends from the year gone by are melted down and added to the batch of beeswax from Tasha's own hives, from which she dips the tapers that will briefly flicker on the family Christmas tree.

Then, as soon as the calendar is turned to December, the holiday season is officially launched. On the first Sunday in the month a wreath of pine and boxwood is suspended from the kitchen ceiling by scarlet ribbons that once garlanded the aisles at Tasha's parents' wedding, and the first of four candles is lit; another candle will be lit each Sunday of the month. In the weeks that follow, an hour or more each day is devoted to the coming festivities: shelling almonds; gathering cedar, pine, fir and other greenery in the woods; and collecting chunks of maple, for only it will do when Tasha bakes her special Dundee cakes in the old-fashioned wood-burning oven next to the hearth.

A favorite task is decorating gingerbread ornaments for the tree, as well as much smaller ones for the dolls' house. Tasha cuts the figures freehand, so of course they are no ordinary gingerbread boys and girls but owls, fish, rams, and other fanciful creatures. With paper cones filled with glossy eggwhite and powdered sugar frosting, she adds the final touches—feathers on the gingerbread owls and scales on the gingerbread fish.

Each day the anticipation builds as the 25th approaches. All four of Tasha's children and her 11 grandchildren have come to the farmhouse for the holiday. Everyone is up early on Christmas Eve morning, for all the preparations must be finished by afternoon teatime.

Then, as the light wanes to purple dusk, the family gathers for the dolls' Christmas party, a diversion the

Tasha Tudor's home deep in the Vermont hills was built by her son. At age seventy-four, she still tends to many of the daily chores of a farm, and even splits her own wood. Here she tells two of her corgis, whose inquisitive nature inspired her Corgiville Fair books, that she is off to town for some last-minute Christmas shopping.

author created for her children when they were young. Their house sits on top of the Christmas chest, and in its parlor wait Emma and other members of the family.

Even the author's grown sons eagerly await the party— "because the dolls give the nicest presents of all," she says slyly. The dolls also receive wonderful gifts from the family each year, among them minuscule brass figurines, a harp for Emma, and a set of wooden bowls and spoons that one of Tasha's grandchildren carved painstakingly out of driftwood one rainy summer afternoon.

Now it is time to attend to the tree. It is brought into the house on the day before Christmas, and Tasha and her youngest son are in charge of trimming it; no one else is allowed to see it until after dinner on Christmas Day. Some of the ornaments have been in Tasha's family since 1858,

including mercury glass balls from Germany, heavy and stuffed with cotton ("If you drop them they don't break, like modern Christmas balls").

In preparation for dinner, the shelves of the china closet are emptied of the finest of everything, down to finger bowls floating with festive leaves of scented geranium. Dinner is wonderful, but it is difficult not to rush through in anticipation of the unveiling of the tree.

Then, at last, dinner is over. A Swiss music box plays a familiar medley of waltzes, the candles on the tree are lit, the door is opened, and the tree is revealed in all its gleaming wonder, the honeyed fragrance of the candles filling the air. All join hands around the tree to sing carols as another magnificent Tasha Tudor Christmas comes to its radiant grande finale.

*W*hen *Tasha Tudor's four children were young, the oldest no more than ten, she invented the Christmas Eve afternoon dolls' party (opposite) to keep them occupied while she attended to the last-minute preparations. A dollmaker since her childhood, Tasha eventually created an entire doll "family." The author decorates the dolls' house for Christmas with the same tender attention she pays to the rest of her world at holiday time.* The *household celebrates St. Nicholas's birthday (above): On December 6, a tea party in the keeping room—for the real people in the family—marks the start of the season's festivities at the farmhouse. The mantel is garlanded with boughs of spruce brought in from the surrounding woods. Candlelight and an open fire make the room fairly glow.*

CHAPTER THREE

The Holly and The Ivy

Just before Christmas, a green lacy vine

called running cedar appeared in the woods

around Freetown and we would

gather yards and yards of it.

We draped everything in the house with it . . .

Edna Lewis
Joy in Freetown

Spring tulips, summer roses, fall

chrysanthemums — each season's bounty

has its own evocative face. But perhaps the most

memory-stirring images

of all are the vibrant

greens of Christmas.

Holly, ivy, cedar, juniper,

and pine never fail to remind us of the abiding

generosity of nature. Tracing a

doorway or mantel, circled into

festive wreaths, or threaded with

ribbons of gold, holiday greens speak of the

warmth of summer's soul,

providing us with such abundance

when we expect it least and

need it most.

Victorians loved the elaborate, and anything that required time and patience was the most revered of all. A creation to be marveled over is this wreath of boxwood (opposite) crested with bouquets of red roses and lady's apples, then ringed with a lace collar that Queen Elizabeth I would have admired. Five bands of gold moiré are stitched together with a fine hand and tipped into golden aglets. ❧ *A simple juniper wreath (above) works Christmas magic as well. Tied with volumes of flocked red ribbon, it dresses up a nineteenth-century cast-iron gas lamp, warming even the coldest December dusk.*

It is because of the Victorians that at Christmastime homes are turned into castles, richly adorned and filled with special cheer. Before the reign of Victoria and her prince consort Albert, Christmas had become a day of fasting and penance. Indeed, the edict of Oliver Cromwell in 1647, which kept shops open and churches closed on Christmas Day, had such a lasting impact that nearly two centuries later Christmas was a subdued holiday. In 1841 when Prince Albert had the first royal Christmas tree set up at Windsor Castle, the country responded with spirit and quickly began to revive old customs with fervor. Instructions appeared in magazines "to strip off the holly berries and use them strung in branches." Halls were decked with ropes of evergreens, and feasting, gift-giving, and merriment returned to December once again.

Some customs changed to suit new Victorian attitudes. Instead of a boar's head, a goose was featured at the feasting. Father Christmas went from a hedonistic fellow drinking from the wassail bowl to the grandfatherly figure illustrated by Thomas Nast, still so beloved today. Every type of decoration was eagerly copied, from elaborate examples of Victorian ribbonery and needlepoint to whimsical paper ornaments embossed with gold and silver. If the sun never set on the British Empire, one reason was that so many people from so many far-flung parts of the globe were busy supplying the Victorians' insatiable demand for ornamentation.

The Victorians not only revived the celebration of Christmas, they invented it anew, imbuing the holiday with a sense of fun, drama, and anticipation.

$\mathcal{O}$utside, December's icy snow is whirling about chimneys and piling up on doorsteps, but inside, all is cozy and serene. It is the hearth more than any other part of the home that embodies the warmth and domestic spirit of this holiday. ❧ This exquisitely restored mantelpiece (left) is the focal point of the formal dining room in a Victorian villa. Carefully chosen nineteenth-century antiques—an Egyptian revival clock, beehive candlesticks, and a sterling silver castor set—rest on its dark marble, while red roses and gilt ribbon lend even more luxuriousness to the setting. ❧ Through tiers of lacy curtains (above) and a wreath of acorns and berries, bright tapers mingle with lights—and stars—beyond.

*T*he Tree only came to itself when it was unloaded in a yard, with the other trees, and heard a man say, "This one is perfect; we only want this one!"

Now two servants came, in gay liveries, and carried the Fir Tree into a large, beautiful saloon. All around the walls hung pictures, and by the great stove stood large Chinese vases with lions on the covers. There were rocking chairs, silken sofas, great tables covered with picture books, and toys worth a hundred times a hundred dollars—at least the children said so. And the Fir Tree was put into a great tub filled with sand; but no one could see that it was a tub, for it was hung round with green cloth, and stood on a large, many-colored carpet. Oh, how the Tree trembled! What was to happen now? The servants and the young ladies, also, decked it out. On one branch they hung little nets cut out of colored paper—every net was filled with sweetmeats; golden apples and walnuts hung down as if they grew there; and more than a hundred little candles, red, white, and blue, were fastened to the different boughs. Dolls that looked exactly like real people—the Tree had never seen such before—swung upon the foliage, and high on the summit of the Tree was fixed a tinsel star. It was splendid, particularly splendid.

"This evening," said all, "this evening it will shine."

Hans Christian Andersen
The Fir Tree

CHAPTER FOUR

Honoring Tradition

It was the policy of the good old gentleman

to make his children feel that home

was the happiest place in the world;

and I value this delicious home-feeling

as one of the choicest gifts

a parent can bestow.

Washington Irving
Christmas Eve

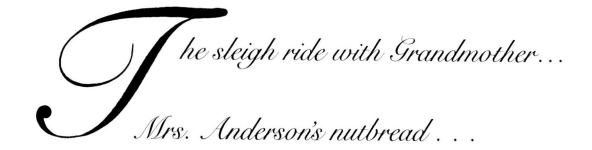

The sleigh ride with Grandmother...

Mrs. Anderson's nutbread . . .

our old Christmas stockings, now frayed

but fiercely protected. The family

album bulging with new photos and old

memories. Christmas Eve dinner with all

the family gathered

around — traditions

at once small and

glorious. The richness

of our heritage, our

family, becomes apparent as the rituals of

December honor the past and are lovingly handed

from generation to generation. In so doing, we

strengthen the present and forge new ties to the

future by keeping these bright memories alive.

Nowhere are Christmas traditions more vividly etched than in those created by families and passed on from generation to generation. As each holiday unfolds, these time-honored rituals take on greater and greater impor- tance, first thrilling us when we are wide-eyed children, later calling forth memories that comfort us in an uncertain world. In families large and small, wise parents and grand- parents delight in providing these precious connections for their children.

In the family of Sandy and David White of Ohio, this sense of intimacy is renewed and enriched each year in a trio of rituals revolving around the decorating of the Christmas tree.

Though Sandy and David both come from families in which only the parents decorated the Christmas tree, in- volving their children in this task became one of the warmest aspects of their holiday tradition. "David and I were thrilled to have these little helping hands," Sandy recalls. "And of course the children loved participating."

The family tree is graced with a very special kind of ornament: homemade cookies in the shapes of favorite storybook characters. "As a child I learned to make the cookies from a lovely lady in our neighborhood," Sandy remembers. "The tops were painted with a mixture of egg white and food coloring. My mother and I spent many happy hours fashioning these cookies. Later, when I had children of my own, I couldn't wait to revive this tradition with them! Hanging them on the tree becomes a very intricate ritual." By now the or- naments have become quite durable.

Another decorating custom plays a major role in the Whites' Christmas. When their three children were young, Sandy and David always returned from trips with spe- cial little presents for each of them—sometimes toys, sometimes souvenirs—that would later serve as ornaments for the tree. "Often they weren't expensive gifts, or even things made to be orna- ments," Sandy explains, "but they were always things that 'looked' like each child." The gifts were carefully tucked away in the "Christmas" closet until a week before the holiday. What makes the tradition even more meaningful is that the children are given their own personal collections when they reach adulthood. Recently, when the Whites' oldest daughter, Carter, was married, Sandy and David presented her with her box of ornaments, one for every trip they had taken since she was a young child. When she and her husband moved to Australia, the box went with her, a rich foundation on which to build Christmases of her own on the other side of the world.

Like a Christmas scene in a small glass globe, the White home perfectly captures the essence of a warm and sharing family holiday. 🕊 *The tree (opposite) is adorned with little gifts and toys given to the children, as well as enameled cookies made by Sandy's mother, a tradition now three generations old.* 🕊 *The treasured silver tray (above) was a wedding gift to Sandy's grandmother, who was married on Christmas Day.*

When we were young, Christmas morning before the presents were opened was the most delicious moment of the entire year. We were up with the birds. We prowled around the tree, poking things and guessing madly. The wait for our parents and grandparents to straggle in was unbearable, but finally they came . . .

They made us wait a little longer while Dad read the Christmas story. After all the excitement and bustle and bursting happiness of the days before Christmas, the reading of Luke's words by the tree suspended us for a moment in time. Did we stop breathing? It seemed so. We sat very quietly . . . while the ancient words flowed over us.

And they came with haste, and found Mary, and Joseph, and the babe lying in a manger. And when they had seen it, they made known abroad the saying which was told them concerning this child. And all they that heard it wondered at those things which were told them by the shepherds. But Mary kept all these things, and pondered them in her heart.

Luke 2:16-19

. . . For a time, after we had grown up and gone our separate spiritual ways, we substituted various readings for Luke's words on Christmas morning. Mom read a few short stories, like "Why the Chimes Rang" and "The Little Match Girl," and one year we each took a part and read the Christmas morning scene from Little Women. *But the substitutes never really worked. We missed the Christmas story, with its words worn silky smooth from constant use, the images and ideas connecting us to Christmases in the past. Now we're back to having Dad read the Christmas story, and as he reads, I can see us around the tree thirty-some years ago with the littlest girls sitting on Grandpa's lap. And I can imagine that at Burkhalter Christmases many years from now, we'll have our own grandchildren in our laps. And as the Christmas story is read, we'll always hear it in Dad's voice.*

Holly J. Burkhalter
The Four Midwestern Sisters' Christmas Book

When interior designer Donald Smith fell in love with his 1848 Georgian-style house in the old river town of Albany, Indiana, it was like the meeting of two souls, one old, one young, reaching across time to join forces. A self-confessed romantic, Donald adored the graciousness of the house and set out to restore it to the elegance it once possessed.

A true labor of love, the painstaking process of bringing out the beauty of this home began with the dining room, a place where Donald could display not only his skills and expertise, but also provide a setting that reflected his boundless hospitality. Mantelpieces were scraped and sanded, moldings restored, walls papered with a delicate red and green chinoiserie pattern, windows shuttered and draped with swags. Along the way Donald decided to forgo the use of electricity in the room entirely: "The space was so romantic that I knew I wanted my guests to dine in the soft reflection of candlelight. Everyone loves it," he adds proudly. "It's always flattering, but never more so than on Christmas Eve."

In keeping with the Victorian spirit of that night, the room is ablaze with the glow from the fireplace and scores of white candles in gleaming candelabra. Antique silver and crystal stemware sparkle in the firelight. Guests are led from one delight to another—cordials are served first in a candlelit corner, dessert served last from a three-tiered stand piled high with sweets. Long after the meal's end, the diners linger, brandy glasses in hand, caught in the spell of this generous host and the magic he re-creates from a lovely, gentle era.

An exquisite brass chandelier (opposite) holds ten candles aloft, illuminating the table below like a stage setting in an elegant play. At Christmas the room is enhanced with fresh flowers, iridescent ribbon, and ivy.

A wreath of fresh roses and hydrangeas (above) seems to be dancing circles around a cluster of brightly flickering votive candles dressed for the occasion with gold foil stars.

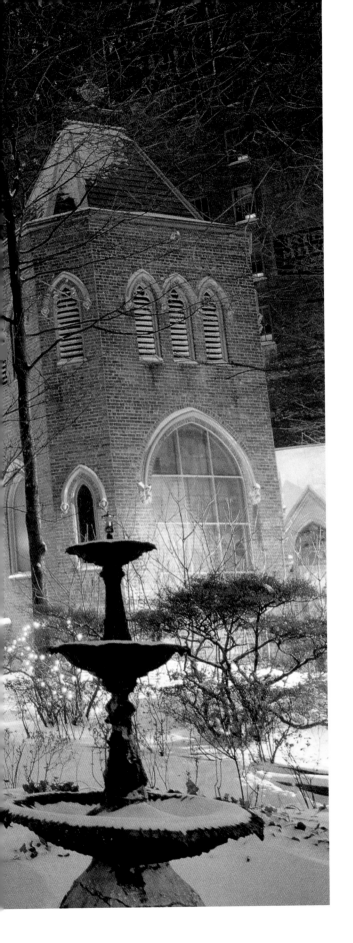

Deep within the canyons of New York City, a tiny jewel sparkles brilliantly in the pristine winter night. It is the Little Church Around the Corner, vibrant with the beauty and joy of the Christmas season. Since its founding in the 1840's, the church has won a devoted following by promoting good will and understanding in the city's varied neighborhoods. Officially known as the Church of the Transfiguration, its reputation for graciousness and hospitality has made it a favorite of people of all faiths, who often come to think of it as "their" church. One group in particular made the Little Church its own: Actors, whose profession made them social outcasts in the nineteenth century, found such a warm welcome here that over the years many have bequeathed the church exquisite gifts like this marble choirboy sculpted in 1871 (above).

As enchanting as the Little Church is all year, at no time is it more magical than on Christmas Eve (left). Magnificent stained-glass windows shimmer like gems, while thousands of lights glow in the snow-covered courtyard. On this night, when the church is filled with glimmering candlelight and the air with caroling, a host of marble angels seems to join in the singing to lift the hearts of all who seek peace and serenity.

CHAPTER FIVE

The Spirit of Romance

May you have the gladness of Christmas

Which is hope;

The spirit of Christmas

Which is peace;

The heart of Christmas

Which is love.

Ada V. Hendricks

To fall in love at any time is to be blessed, but to fall in love at Christmas is to receive an extraordinary gift, for this is the holiday when all  emotions are heightened. A tingle becomes a thrill, happiness turns to enchantment, affection deepens to love. The essence of romance lies

at the heart of Christmas,

with its promise of devotion

and renewal. For knowing

lovers, the sharing of the

holiday ritual, in moments private and intimate,

can only enrich the

joys of the season

and the ties of love.

The table is set, the candles glowing, the fire gently burning. The air is laden with the aroma of rosemary topiaries and mantel garlands. Everything is perfect for a private evening for two, filled with tranquillity and intimate conversation.

Christmas is a holiday that plays over all the senses, but perhaps the most evocative is that of smell. Simple fragrances like those of freshly baked gingerbread cookies enthrall us as youngsters. As adults we delight in the sophisticated aromas of herbs. More precious and rare than the extravagant blooms of summer, herbs take on a special cachet in the cold winter months, almost defying Nature with their romantic spirit. Sturdy lavender, sage, and santalina perfume the air from their sunny windowsill perches; pine, juniper, and bayberries combine their distinctive scents in glorious potpourris.

But perhaps the herb most closely associated with this holiday is rosemary. Soft and pliable, it is used in ways as myriad as the pleasures it provides. Bushy lengths can be bound into wreaths, or gracefully draped from a mantelpiece. Their pinelike boughs can be placed about the house in bouquets with fresh white lilacs, roses, or lilies. As an extra note of elegance, romantic topiaries are especially lovely set out in a room like treasured trees from a miniature forest. Decorating with rosemary honors traditions past and deepens the ties to loved ones, for this is the herb Sir Thomas More believed to be "sacred to remembrance, and therefore to friendship."

Beside a glowing fire, a rosemary topiary, dainty enough to rest upon a table, oversees an intimate candlelit dinner for lovers, while rosemary garlands with creamy white roses and freesia spread languorously across the lacy cover of a snow-white mantelpiece.

Like the church chimes on Christmas morning that pierce our hearts with their beauty, the haunting fragrances of holiday flowers and herbs arouse our memories and stir our souls. Pungent, musky, or sweet, each is greeted like a dear old friend, returning for the holidays.

More precious because of their rarity, more surprising because of their out-of-season appearance, winter's fresh flowers are a triumph at Christmas. They heighten anticipation and expectation, lend their elegance without restraint. The vitality of their very presence never fails to excite and charm.

Symbols of birth, good fellowship, and love, flowers have traditionally been a joyful part of the holiday celebration. While all flowers are sublime in winter, it is the majesty of red roses that reigns supreme at Christmas. In this season of mistletoe and holly, there are hosts of pleasing ways to use red roses. One of the sweetest is to make crowns to adorn the tresses of favorite little girls, much like the St. Lucia crowns worn by the youngest daughters in Swedish Christmas celebrations. For a memorable Christmas Eve dinner, hand-lettered place cards fashioned from tiny sweetheart roses and fragrant pine guide guests to their seats. Roses are spectacularly flattering to winter colorings: worn as a necklace, pinned on a white lacy collar, or woven into a hair ornament, their deep red glow casting a blush on the cheeks of young beauties. Even a favorite pet can be graced by this regal flower when a perfect red rose is tied on its collar.

And nothing fills a home more with the beauty and fragrance of the season than roses—dozens of small bouquets in crystal stem glasses, alone or in groupings in front of every mirror in the house, or scattered in pretty china plates and bowls, like love notes left around the house. Merry wreaths and exuberant swags emblazoned with colorful red roses welcome Christmas visitors. When combined with herbs, they delight with their delicate scents as well as their outer beauty. Holiday potpourris of juniper, bay leaves, cinnamon, and pine cones become memorable with the addition of red rosebuds. Tucking the rose stems into florists' vials will keep their blooms pristine for days. Like ruby gemstones in precious settings, red roses placed among the boughs of the Christmas tree seem to blaze with fire.

Roses are unsurpassed for their romantic beauty (above and opposite). Nestled atop bowls brimming with potpourris, their perfume blends into the spirited herbal air. Like old-fashioned boutonnieres, brilliant red roses are elegant entwined in the greenery of wreaths and garlands. Even the most charming of Victorian traditions, the tabletop tree, grows more resplendent when graced with this royal red flower.

That most Victorian of Victorian customs—the Christmas tree—grew out of the great love shared between a husband and wife. Apart from the fact that the wife was Victoria, Queen of England, and her husband, Albert, the prince consort, these were two ordinary lovers smitten with each other, their young family, and the celebration of Christmas itself.

Theirs was one of history's great love stories. In 1839 young Queen Victoria, faced with the obligation of selecting a mate and perpetuating the royal dynasty, summoned all the eligible princes of Europe for consideration. Since royal alliances rarely produced love matches, Victoria understandably viewed this endeavor as a "dreadful" necessity. Imagine her great joy when instead of being forced to enter into a businesslike arrangement, she fell passionately in love with the handsome Prince Albert of Saxony. The affection was returned by Albert, and not long after the two were married.

Royal family life flourished, and by 1841 Victoria and Albert were the parents of two small children. That

Christmas, a homesick Albert had small evergreen trees shipped from his ancestral home of Coburg, Germany, to Windsor Castle, where the family was celebrating the holiday. Queen Victoria, ever eager to please Albert, had one tree placed on a table in a spotlight of honor. Fruit, flowers, garlands of gilt and ribbons, birds, and glass ornaments decorated its graceful boughs. At its crown, a beautiful angel with hovering wings blessed this little family. On Christmas Eve, tiny flaming tapers shed a delicate light upon this first Victorian Christmas tree. The Tree of Love, as it was called, became the centerpiece of the royal family's yearly Christmas celebrations.

The custom immediately caught on at Court, and soon captured the imagination of the general population. A loving tradition was born.

Even today, on the threshold of another century, Victoria and Albert's ideals and values continue to be venerated. The Christmas tree remains the symbolic center of family celebrations, inspired by the devotion of one couple whose love for each other was as glorious as the titles they bore.

This majestic Christmas tree (opposite) could have graced the parlor of Queen Victoria herself. Its boughs display a wealth of antique ornaments and holiday images dear to Victorian hearts. Strand upon strand of golden beads arc across the tree in delicate curves, and little gilt ribbons are tied to the ends of the branches. High atop the tree's crown, a hand-carved angel (above) beams with benevolence, sheltering all under her outstretched wings.

Intricate as the work of Jack Frost on a windowpane, luxuriant lace and fine antique linen capture all the loveliness of the season. Whether soft, crisp, starched, or supple, new or antique, their many faces are a timeless reflection of the beauty and richness of Christmas images lovingly remembered.

Victorians considered lacemaking a gentle art. Even the smallest bit of lace is a testament to the patience and precision of its maker. Today, the highest value is placed on such handmade antique lace. Particularly precious are family heirlooms; fragile and delicate though they may be, they forge strong ties to the past and equally lasting ties to the future.

This is a season made for lace. As beautiful to behold as it is to touch, lace endows every room with a romantic, festive feeling. A gauzy piece across the top of a doorway frame creates a heavenly entryway; a strip on a Christmas stocking on the mantelpiece lends a delicate air. Ribbons of antique lace can be used as tiebacks for the curtains fastened with Grandmother's garnet brooch or looped over a doorknob to hold a tiny tussy-mussy.

Lace provides a radiant backdrop against which the greens, fruits, berries, and flowers of Christmas can be seen to their most glorious advantage. Pots of amaryllis and paperwhites corseted in poufs of filmy new lace take on a cloudlike air. Holiday arrangements of fruits and flowers beam with a sparkling clarity when viewed against the pristine white of a linen tablecloth. Tiny baskets lined with lace-edged cloths and laden with foil-wrapped candies seem like gifts left in the snow. Hand-sewn bows of starched white lace add a homey Victorian touch to holly and ivy wreaths. Hearths piled with vines and swags of lace draw friends and family near.

The soft glow of candlelight illuminates a scene of exceptional romance (opposite). No bride could be more beautiful, no valentine more extravagant than this holiday table for two gleaming with the finest crystal, silver, and delicate old lace. To fashion this magic moment, two layers of lace tablecloths, one of needlepoint, the other a richly embroidered cutwork lace, are caught up by a nosegay of pure white roses, ivy, cherries, and a sprig of rose hips.
Like an illustration of a long-ago Christmas, this fine cutwork linen tablecloth (above) provides a magical transport into a world of beauty and nostalgia. Special holiday tableware shines against the backdrop of its snowy splendor, while swags of creamy white roses swirl around the base of lustrous candlesticks.

Whaat shall my true love
Have from me
To pleasure his Christmas
Wealthily?
The partridge has flown
From our pear tree.
Flown with our summers
Are the swans and the geese.
Milkmaids and drummers
Would leave him little peace.
I've no gold ring
And no turtle dove,
So what can I bring
To my true love?

A coat for the drizzle
Chosen at the store;
A saw and a chisel
For mending the door;
A pair of red slippers
To slip on his feet;
Three striped neckties;
Something sweet.

He shall have all
I can best afford—
No pipers piping,
No leaping lord,
But a fine fat hen
For his Christmas board;
Two pretty daughters
(Versed in the role)
To be worn like pinks
In his buttonhole;
And the tree of my heart
With its calling linnet—
My evergreen heart
And the bright bird in it.

Phyllis McGinley
All the Days of Christmas

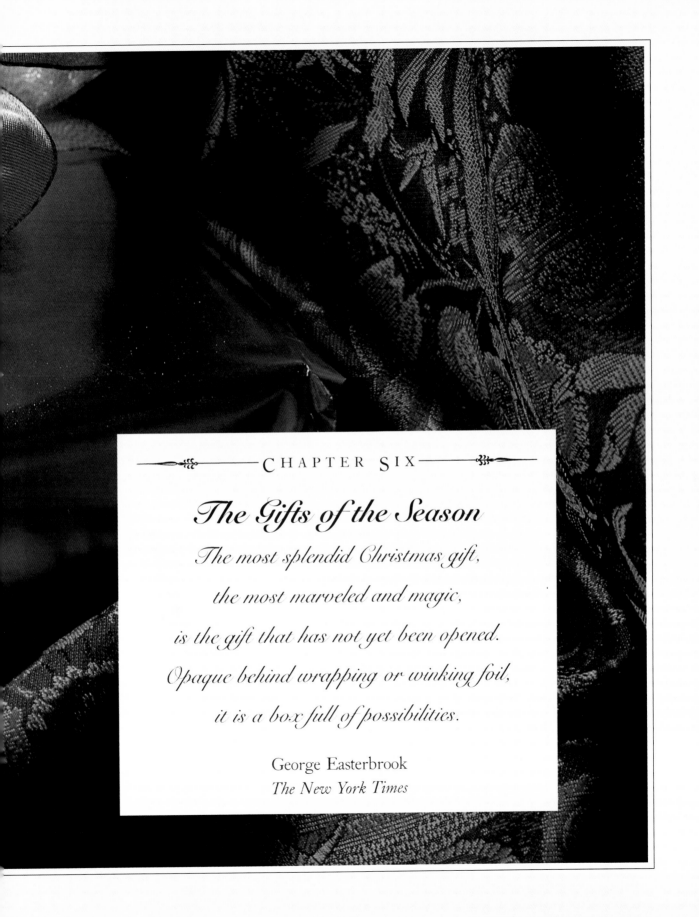

CHAPTER SIX

The Gifts of the Season

The most splendid Christmas gift,

the most marveled and magic,

is the gift that has not yet been opened.

Opaque behind wrapping or winking foil,

it is a box full of possibilities.

George Easterbrook
The New York Times

The generosity of the season

is the giving of time, that

most precious commodity — the hours spent

searching for the perfect

present or the special

ingredient, the trimming

and untangling, the wrapping and shelling and

roasting and polishing. And out of all this

labor and time

come the true

gifts of Christmas:

the blessing of

hearth and home, the strengthening of family

ties, and the unfolding of the few days that are,

as Shakespeare wrote, "so

hallowed and so gracious."

Santa Claus. The name alone sends a chill of anticipation down the spine. What child hasn't pressed her nose to a windowpane, peering into the sky for a glimpse of Santa's sleigh and reindeer? He is a symbol more endearing than a host of cupids, Easter bunnies, and fairy godmothers. He has first place in everyone's affections for two wonderful reasons—parents encourage children to believe in him, and he never fails to excite and delight.

Is there anyone else who has the power to look inside a child's heart and fulfill his secret desires? Is there anyone else who gives without getting in return year after year? Only Santa. Santa is the spirit of giving itself, and of course, it wouldn't be Christmas without him.

The tradition of midwinter gift-giving goes back to the ancients. As day by day the sun climbed higher in the sky, it was considered good luck to be generous to one and all by giving presents that were not just tokens of affection but an attempt to surprise the recipient. Over the centuries, that spirit of generosity has been embodied in the figure of the gentle, white-bearded St. Nicholas, a fourth-century Turkish bishop who became known as the patron saint and guardian of children. His birthday, December 6, was celebrated for centuries, and in some European countries the custom of leaving secret gifts for children on the eve of St. Nicholas Day is still practiced today.

In the early eighteenth century, Clement C. Moore's immortal poem "A Visit from St. Nicholas" introduced American children to a new image. St. Nicholas became a "right jolly old elf" riding through the air on his miniature sleigh drawn by eight tiny reindeer. It wasn't until later in the century, as the Victorian ideal of home and family took hold, that Santa took on the wise, grandfatherly aspect so beloved today. This modern ideal sprang from the pen of cartoonist Thomas Nast, whose illustrations frequently appeared in the popular magazine *Harper's Weekly*. In 1863 Nast transformed Santa into that much adored figure, with his twinkling eyes and cherubic, portly figure. Wrapped in a fur-trimmed red robe, with shiny black belt and boots, his fluffy white beard and funny little cap, the enduring persona of Santa links generation to generation—so much so that young children go to bed on Christmas Eve dreaming about the same Santa as did their parents, grandparents, and great-grandparents.

Later, from the perspective of adulthood, Santa Claus comes to represent more than toy trains and dolls. His greatest gift is one that lasts all year—the joy of giving. Despite crowded department stores, families everywhere plunge into the mad joy of shopping, determined to find just exactly the right presents for loved ones. It's Christmastime. It's everyone's turn to become Santa.

Children's gifts are not just for children, as these patchwork teddy bears (above) can attest. Made by Florida craftswomen, they are presents cherished by adult collectors. A paper and cotton Santa, an enduring example of Victorian scrap art, nestles among antique ornaments on a richly decorated tree (opposite).

Swaths of delicate fabrics like silk, dotted Swiss, moiré, and netting, surrounded with snippets of antique lace and satin ribbons and topped with small bunches of flowers or boughs of holiday greens, create gift wraps so lovely they become gifts in themselves. (Opposite) Crinkly silk moiré wraps this certain-to-be-cherished gift. A corsage of holiday greens, Spanish moss, and blackberry twigs becomes the heart of its generous bow. (This page) A trio of gifts is enveloped in the pure elegance of clouds of white netting and lace bows. Sprigs of pine and rose nosegays provide the loveliest of finishing touches.

Claremont, December 24, 1836

I awoke after 7 and got up at 8. After 9 breakfasted, at a little after 10 we left Kensington with dearest Lehzen, Lady Conroy and—Dashy! and reached Claremont at a quarter to 12. Played and sang. At 2 dearest Lehzen, Victoire and I went out, and came home at 20 minutes past 8. No one was stirring about the gipsy encampment except George, which I was sorry for as I was anxious to know how our poor friends were, after this bitterly cold night. Played and sang. Received from dearest, best Lehzen as a Christmas box two lovely little Dresden China figures, two pair of lovely little chased gold buttons, a small lovely button with an angel's head which she used to wear herself, and a pretty music book; from good Louis a beautiful piece of Persian stuff for an album; and from Victoire and Emily Gardiner a small box worked by themselves. Wrote my journal, went down to arrange Mamma's table for her. At 6 we dined. Mr. Edward Byrne and Mr. Conroy stayed here. Mr. Byng is going to stay here a night or two. Very soon after dinner Mamma sent for us into the gallery, where all the things were arranged on different tables. From my dear Mamma I received a beautiful massive gold buckle in the shape of two serpents; a lovely little delicate gold chain with turquoise clasp; a lovely coloured sketch of dearest Aunt Louise by Partridge copied from the picture he brought and so like her; 3 beautiful drawings by Munn, one lovely seaview by Peser and one cattle piece by Cooper (all coloured), 3 prints, a book called Finden's Tableau, Heath's Picturesque Annual, Ireland; both these are very pretty; Friendship's offering and the English Annual for 1837, the Holy Land illustrated beautifully, two handkerchiefs, a very pretty black satin apron trimmed with red velvet, and two almanacks. I am very thankful to my dear Mamma for all these very pretty things. From dear Uncle Leopold a beautiful turquoise ring; from the Queen a fine piece of Indian gold tissue, and from Sir J. Conroy a print. I gave my dear Lehzen a green morocco jewel case, and the Picturesque Annual; Mamma gave her a shawl, a pair of turquoise earrings, an annual, and handkerchiefs. I then took Mamma to the Library where my humble table was arranged; I gave her a bracelet made of my hair, and the Keepsake, and Oriental Annual. I stayed up til eleven!

From Queen Victoria's Journal

Steeped in the tradition of centuries past, the artful use of fruit, vines, nuts, and berries is a seasonal reminder of how rewarding it is to transform the seemingly ordinary into the truly exquisite. (Opposite) Small delicate delights are created when natural materials are joined with the opulence of beautiful antiques: Lush vintage fabric meets shining fruits and berries in a sumptuous counterpoint of colors and textures; leather-bound volumes burnished with the patina of age turn into extraordinary presents when tied up with red velvet and peppercorns; even simple wire baskets filled with fruit and trailing plants become lovely centerpiece gifts. ❧ (Above) The rosy red of a clutch of berries glows like garnets next to the luster of a cherished silver vase.

𝒥n many families, the small jewels that hang on the tree are almost reluctantly removed each year following Twelfth Night, carefully returned to a growing number of boxes marked "FRAGILE: CHRISTMAS ORNAMENTS" and stored in the recesses of a closet well out of harm's way. Next December, once again, the boxes will be brought out and set on the dining room table. As if for the first time, each ornament is rediscovered, and great care is taken not to lose a few bits of crystal or glass in the crumpled-up piles of last year's newspaper. The great joy of giving and receiving an ornament is that it can be admired over and over again, carrying with it the memory of a special

Christmas and a special association, both of which increase immeasurably in value with time. ❧ *This tree (opposite) is encrusted with a breathtaking array of vintage Dresden ornaments, each one a perfect gift in itself. Made of silver- or gold-faced paper, they are richly embossed and filigreed, with great care and attention to even the smallest detail. Joining the collection are small ancestral portraits in ornate silver frames.* ❧ *A miniature world of ornaments (above) reflects the whimsy and merriment of Victorian life. Among the treasures are antique Santas hurrying along, carriages, and musical instruments.*

CHAPTER SEVEN

From a Victorian Table

The table was literally loaded

with good cheer,

and presented the epitome of country abundance,

in this season of overflowing abundance.

Mary Howitt
Pictorial Calendar of the Seasons

*S*o many of the joys of Christmas are sensory, and nowhere do the pleasures of the senses come together more richly than at the table. Aromas associated only with this season — a steaming plum pudding or a burst of freshly ground cardamom — bring on a heady rush of holiday memories.

At Christmas dinner, we

enjoy the dishes that

tradition is made of:

The menu is always what we expect and what

we have come to love, as each glorious feast

mirrors those of our parents

and their parents before them.

I never lived near my grandparents Ward, and so I don't imagine that my family celebrated Christmas at their house more than three or four times during my boyhood. But theirs was the definitive Christmas against which all others are still measured in my family. . . .

"Now go ahead and start in," Grandpa always told us, poking at the air with a flesh fork as he doled out the slices of breast meat that seemed to fall from his knife like pages from a book. "Don't wait for me. It'll just get cold."

And so we would all start in, passing the cranberries over the china and silver and crystal . . . but by the time Grandpa had finally served himself, and all the fixings had been passed around again for his benefit, his eagle eye would alight on a grandson's already empty plate.

"Geoff? It looks as though you could do with a little more turkey."

"Yes, thank you, Grandpa," my brother would say, passing back his plate. "It's all delicious."

"That's the boy," Grandpa replied, bending over the shredded bird. "Of course," he muttered, pouting slightly, "I haven't had my first bite yet."

We would debate the vices and virtues of Eisenhower and Oberlin faculty politics and the fruit harvest just past and the route we took to get there while we consumed the white meat and dark meat and the yams and creamed onions and gravy and stuffing and cranberries and relishes, and then the plum pudding flaming blue and gold, with hard sauce so braced with brandy that it made my sister's eyes water. And when the dishes were done and the narcotic of turkey and champagne and hard sauce had kicked in, the adults dozed and we children dawdled, sated, in the far-flung reaches of the house.

Andrew Ward
The Christmas Feast

When guests are served dinner at the Victorian inn run by Ronald and Susan Gibson in Union City, Michigan, they dine on exquisitely prepared foods based on authentic Victorian recipes. From the cheddar soup to the plum pudding, "the foods are rooted in the era," explains the host, "and I mean that literally. Everything we serve must be fresh, and much of it is grown in our own organic gardens, often from the nineteenth-century strains of seeds available in specialty catalogs. When people eat here they can't believe how special even the simplest food tastes. Once you've eaten something as ordinary as home-prepared applesauce or tasted herbs grown in your own garden, you don't ever want to buy the commercial stuff again."

Ronald Gibson has always had great reverence for the past. His childhood Christmases were special times for him, reuniting elderly grandparents, uncles and aunts, and cousins. When he and Susan married, they resolved to make their holiday celebrations rich with tradition. Ronald began what turned out to be an absolutely wonderful literary voyage into the past, buying old books from the Victorian era. "The more I read, the more I became intrigued with the way Christmases had been resurrected by the Victorians." Ten years ago the Gibsons bought an 1870's villa in the Italianate style and began doing much of the restoring themselves. When the job was done, they decided to turn it into an inn, furnished with all the

wonderful Victoriana they had been collecting for years. The hosts, who had always prepared traditional English Christmas dinners for friends and family, began to offer this Dickensian feast to guests at the inn.

As they started experimenting in earnest with Victorian recipes, they found instructions for a "handful" or a "goodly amount" often meant many failed dishes before they achieved success. They also had to make adjustments for the modern palate. "The Victorians used huge amounts of cinnamon, and how they loved their fat, dipping their bread into little dishes of goose grease. No wonder they had gout!" comments Ronald.

A Victorian Christmas dinner wouldn't be Victorian without a goose, but preparing one they liked turned out to be a difficult task. "Like most people, we had tasted goose and not liked it because of the way it was prepared," Ronald explains. "It took some time to figure it out: You have to make sure that the goose doesn't sit directly on the bottom of the pan. We cook ours in electric roasting pans because they're easiest to control, and there's a lot of steaming going on the entire time, which eliminates the grease."

Of all the recipes they adapted, none required more research and experimentation than plum pudding; it took six years before the Gibsons came up with one that met all their criteria for esthetics as well as taste. It is also the most intriguing recipe. "The fun thing about plum pudding is, it has everything but plums in it," says Ronald. "There

A simple cheddar soup launches the Victorian adventure in eating at the Gibsons' Christmas table. The couple experimented with many nineteenth-century recipes for this traditional first course but found each one too strongly flavored with cheese. After many attempts they came up

with a dish that is subtly flavored with leeks, celery, dry mustard, and bacon and is garnished with fresh chives, rosemary, and flowering borage. Guests at their inn enjoy fresh herbs all winter long, supplied by a neighbor who keeps a large indoor herb garden.

must be a total of sixteen ingredients, but of all the recipes and all the books I've looked at, not one called for plums. It's a Victorian joke." They looked for substitutes for the traditional suet, dismissing the notion that its slow melting gives the pudding its feathery texture. They found that the same effect can be achieved with cold bits of unsalted butter. They also use apples, another nontraditional ingredient, and hot, fresh-pressed apple cider to plump the raisins before steaming.

The presentation of the pudding is a moment of high drama: "The Victorians loved to ignite things, and now I know why," says Ronald. "When you carry in a hot and steaming plum pudding with its blue flame of ignited brandy, it's just a magnificent finale."

People from the area as well as weekend guests from all over the country can enjoy everything from Christmas teas to complete Christmas dinners on six weekends starting at Thanksgiving. "I have always felt that one of the small contributions we have been able to make at the inn is to expose people to these jolly old customs," Ronald says.

Do they ever get tired of Christmas? "Oh, no," Ronald says, a little surprised. "Not when we see the looks on people's faces when they taste our goose and plum pudding."

Inveterate collectors of Victoriana, the Gibsons use their most resplendent pieces at Christmas. The stacking compotes of pressed glass are remarkably delicate pieces for their size. The Old Country Rose china pieces, which are used only during the holiday season, are from Royal Dalton's Prince Albert collection.

A Christmas Feast

Cream of Cheddar Soup

*Stuffed Goose
with Forcemeat and Chestnut Stuffing*

Roasted Potatoes

Purée of Fresh Fennel and Broccoli

Rum Butter Plum Pudding

Country Wassail

CREAM OF CHEDDAR SOUP

For many of us, Christmas dinner represents the ultimate wintertime feast, and this rich, creamy soup makes a lovely starter.

Makes 8 to 10 servings

½ cup unsalted butter (1 stick)
1 cup finely chopped celery
1 cup sliced leeks
⅓ cup all-purpose flour
2 teaspoons dry mustard
¼ teaspoon salt
¼ teaspoon pepper
1½ cups chicken stock
2 cups half-and-half
2 cups milk
*2 cups finely shredded sharp Cheddar
  cheese (8 ounces)*
4 slices bacon, cooked crisp and crumbled
*Whole chives and herb flowers, for
  garnish*

1. In a heavy 3-quart saucepan, melt the butter over medium-high heat. Add the celery and leeks. Cook for 8 to 10 minutes, stirring often, until the vegetables are tender.

2. Stir in the flour, dry mustard, salt, and pepper until blended. Gradually stir in the chicken broth and cook until the mixture thickens and bubbles, stirring constantly. Lower the heat to medium and continue to cook, stirring, for 1 minute more.

3. Gradually stir the half-and-half and the milk into the thickened broth. Cover and cook gently for about 10 minutes until the soup is heated through, stirring occasionally.

4. Reduce the heat to low. Gradually stir in the cheese until melted.

5. Stir in the bacon just before serving. Ladle the soup into warmed cups and garnish each with 3 or 4 whole chives and herb flowers.

STUFFED GOOSE

The stuffing for this delectable goose blends chestnuts, mushrooms, and pecans with more traditional ingredients such as onions, apples, celery, and pork sausage. The redolent mixture is seasoned with sage, parsley, thyme, rosemary, and basil.

Makes 6 servings

1 domestic goose, 8 to 10 pounds
3 cups water
½ teaspoon salt
¼ teaspoon black pepper

Forcemeat and Chestnut Stuffing:
¾ pound whole fresh chestnuts
1 tablespoon unsalted butter
*2 unpeeled tart cooking apples, cored
  and chopped*
1 tablespoon sugar
½ pound bulk pork sausage
1 cup finely chopped celery
1 cup finely chopped onion
1 cup small whole button mushrooms
1 cup chopped pecans
¼ cup chopped fresh parsley
*2 tablespoons chopped fresh sage or
  2 teaspoons dried or rubbed sage*
*2 tablespoons chopped fresh thyme or
  2 teaspoons dried thyme*
*1 tablespoon chopped fresh rosemary or
  1 teaspoon dried rosemary*
*1 tablespoon chopped fresh basil or
  1 teaspoon dried basil*
*14 slices firm-textured bread, crusts
  removed, cubed (about 8 cups)*
1½ cups cooked wild rice
1½ cups cooked brown rice
*1½ cups finely shredded Cheddar cheese
  (6 ounces)*
3 large eggs, beaten

Fresh herbs, for garnish
Apple slices or lady apples, for garnish

1. Remove the giblets and neck from the goose, rinse thoroughly, and set aside. Discard the liver. Rinse the goose thoroughly, removing as much fat as possible from the body cavity.

2. Pat the goose dry with paper towels. Cover and refrigerate.

3. In a large saucepan combine the goose giblets and neck, water, salt, and pepper and bring to a boil. Lower the heat, cover the pan, and simmer for 1 to 1½ hours or until the giblets are tender.

4. Strain and reserve the broth. Discard the neck. Chop the giblets and set them aside.

To make the Stuffing:

1. Preheat the oven to 400°F.

2. With a sharp knife, cut a small slit in each chestnut shell. Put the chestnuts on a baking sheet and roast for 15 to 20 minutes.

3. Remove the chestnuts from the oven and set them aside to cool.

4. In a small skillet, melt the butter over medium heat. Add the apples and sauté for 3 to 4 minutes or until almost tender. Remove the apples from the heat and sprinkle with the sugar. Set aside.

5. In a large skillet, combine the sausage, celery, onion, and mushrooms and cook over medium-high heat for about 10 minutes or until the sausage is cooked through and the vegetables are tender, stirring often. Remove from the heat and drain off the fat. Put the sausage mixture in a 6-quart bowl.

6. Peel the cooled chestnuts and chop them coarsely. Add the chestnuts to the sausage mixture together with the pecans, chopped giblets, parsley, sage, thyme, rosemary, and basil. Mix together well.

7. Add the bread cubes, sautéed apples, cooked wild rice, cooked brown rice, cheese, and eggs. Mix together well. Stir in ½ cup of the reserved goose broth to moisten the stuffing.

To prepare the Goose:

1. Preheat the oven to 450°F. Season the body cavity of the goose with salt. Prick the skin (not the meat) all over with a large fork.

2. Lightly spoon some stuffing into the neck cavity. Pull the neck skin over the stuffing and fasten securely to the back of the goose with a small skewer. Lightly spoon some stuffing into the body cavity. Truss the goose. Put the remaining stuffing into a buttered 2-quart casserole, cover, and refrigerate.

3. Put the goose, breast side down, on a rack in a large roasting pan. Pour 1 cup of the goose broth into the pan. Roast the goose for 20 minutes.

4. Baste the goose with pan drippings. Lower the oven temperature to 350°F. Turn the goose, breast side up, and continue to roast for 20 to 23 minutes per pound or until the thermometer registers 185°F. During roasting baste the goose with pan drippings occasionally, and remove the fat that accumulates in the pan.

5. Bake the stuffing in the covered casserole during the last 45 minutes of roasting time.

6. Remove the goose from the oven. Place on a serving platter, cover with foil, and let stand for 15 minutes before carving.

7. Garnish with fresh herbs and apple slices or lady apples. Serve the goose with the baked stuffing, as well as the stuffing in the cavities.

ROASTED POTATOES
....

Roasted potatoes are as traditional with roast fowl as bells are with horse-drawn sleighs. These, with the skin left on except for a decorative center strip, are lavishly brushed with butter, then roasted to a tender turn.

Makes 8 servings

2½ pounds red new potatoes (about 8 medium or 16 small potatoes)
3 tablespoons unsalted butter, softened
1 to 2 teaspoons coarse salt

1. Preheat the oven to 350° F.

2. Peel a narrow strip around the center of each potato. Prick the potatoes with a fork.

3. Generously spread each potato with butter and sprinkle with salt. Wrap and seal each in a small piece of foil.

4. Put the foil-wrapped potatoes on a baking sheet. Bake until fork-tender, about 40 minutes for small potatoes, or 1 hour for medium potatoes.

PUREE OF FRESH FENNEL AND BROCCOLI

················

The distinctive taste of fennel marries nicely with the mellow, more familiar flavor of broccoli, whose dark green color stands out in bold contrast to the lighter hue of the pureed fennel. Served alongside the goose, the pureed green vegetables provide a good balance of flavors and textures that round out the Christmas meal. Fennel, which looks rather like squashed celery with feathery, frondlike leaves, is readily available in supermarkets and at greengrocers everywhere.

Makes 6 to 8 servings

1 pound broccoli
2 large bulbs fresh fennel (about 1 pound each)
2 tablespoons (¼ stick) unsalted butter
1 medium onion, chopped (1 cup)
¼ cup heavy cream
Salt
Freshly ground black pepper
1 tablespoon chopped fresh herbs, such as parsley, chives, rosemary, and thyme

1. Cut up the broccoli florets and cut the tender stems into ¼-inch-thick slices. You should have about 4 cups. Blanch the broccoli in boiling water for 3 minutes. Drain and set aside.
2. Remove the fronds and tough outer layers from the fennel. Halve each bulb and remove the cores. Cut the fennel into ¼-inch-thick slices. You should have about 3 cups. Blanch the fennel in boiling water for 5 min-

utes or until tender. Drain and set aside.
3. In a small skillet, melt the butter over medium-high heat. Add the onion and sauté until golden brown, stirring often.
4. Put the cooked fennel in a food processor. Add half the sautéed onion and half the cream, and process until smooth. Stir in salt and pepper to taste. Remove the puree from the processor and mound into a serving dish.
5. Put the cooked broccoli in the food processor. Add the remaining sautéed onion and cream, and process until smooth. Stir in the herbs, and salt and pepper to taste.
6. Make a depression in the center of the fennel puree with the back of a spoon. Mound the broccoli puree in the center of the fennel.

RUM BUTTER PLUM PUDDING

··························

Old English tradition says that plum pudding is the symbol of Christmas. Its roundness represents the good and abundant earth, the decorative holly berries stand for the blood of Christ, and the ignited brandy suggests the flames of hell rapidly burned away as the goodness of the season prevails.

Makes about 8 servings

Plum Pudding:
2 apples, peeled, cored, and chopped
½ cup freshly squeezed orange juice
2 tablespoons freshly squeezed lemon juice
1 cup dark seedless raisins
1 cup chopped candied citrus peel
1 cup dried red tart cherries
½ cup dried currants
1 teaspoon finely grated orange zest
1 teaspoon finely grated lemon zest
½ cup brandy
1 cup all-purpose flour
1 tablespoon baking powder
½ teaspoon ground cinnamon
¼ teaspoon ground cloves
¼ teaspoon ground allspice
½ cup (1 stick) unsalted butter, softened
½ cup packed light brown sugar
3 large eggs

Rum Butter:
½ cup (1 stick) unsalted butter, softened
2 cups confectioners' sugar
3 tablespoons dark rum
1 teaspoon vanilla extract

To make the Plum Pudding:
1. In a large nonreactive (enamel or stainless steel) bowl, toss the apples with the orange juice and lemon juice. Add the raisins, citrus peel, cherries, currants, orange zest, and lemon zest. Stir in the brandy until well mixed. Cover and refrigerate for several hours or up to 1 week, stirring occasionally.
2. In a small bowl, mix together the flour, baking powder, cinnamon, cloves, and allspice. Sift the flour mixture over the fruit mixture and mix well.
3. In the medium bowl of an electric mixer, beat the butter with the brown sugar at medium speed for 5 minutes or until fluffy. Add the eggs,

one at a time, beating well after each addition. Stir into the fruit mixture. The mixture will look curdled.

4. Butter a 2-quart tube-shaped pudding mold. Scrape the batter into the prepared mold and cover tightly with a lid or heavy-duty aluminum foil. Put the mold on a rack or an inverted heatproof saucer in a large saucepan. Pour boiling water into the saucepan to come two thirds up the sides of the mold. Bring to a boil.

5. Lower the heat to medium-low so that the water gently simmers. Cover the saucepan with a tight-fitting lid and steam for 2 hours, adding more boiling water as needed.

6. Remove the pudding mold from the saucepan. Remove the lid and cool the pudding on a rack for at least 1 hour.

COUNTRY WASSAIL
. . . .

The word wassail is from the Anglo-Saxon *waes hael* meaning "be in good health." This potent punch is traditionally served from a very large bowl on Christmas Eve, New Year's Eve, and Twelfth Night to family and friends.

Makes 35 to 40 punch cup servings

Baked Apples:
*8 small baking apples (about 1³/4
    pounds)*
1 cup packed light brown sugar
1/2 teaspoon ground cinnamon
1/4 teaspoon ground nutmeg
1/8 teaspoon ground allspice
1 cup brandy

Wassail:
*3 medium oranges, each cut into
    8 wedges*
1 tablespoon whole cloves
*1 gallon fresh apple cider or natural
    apple juice*
1 quart cranberry juice
2 teaspoons aromatic bitters (optional)
3/4 cup sugar
5 3-inch cinnamon sticks
1 tablespoon whole allspice
2 to 2¹/2 cups dark rum (optional)
Orange slices, for garnish

To make the Baked Apples:
1. Preheat the oven to 350°F.
2. Core the apples but leave on the stems. Peel a strip from around the top of each apple. Put the apples in a large baking dish. Set aside.
3. In a medium saucepan, combine the brown sugar, cinnamon, nutmeg, and allspice. Stir in the brandy. Bring just to a boil over medium-high heat until the sugar dissolves, stirring occasionally.
4. Pour the brandy mixture over the apples. Cover the dish and bake for 25 to 30 minutes or until tender.

To make the Wassail:
1. While the apples are baking, stud the orange wedges with cloves. Set aside.
2. In an 8-quart saucepan, combine the apple cider, cranberry juice, and bitters, if desired. Add the orange wedges, sugar, cinnamon sticks, and allspice. Stirring constantly, bring just to a boil until the sugar dissolves.
3. Lower the heat. Cover and simmer for 10 minutes. Stir in the rum, if desired. Cover and heat through.
4. Strain the hot wassail into a large serving bowl or punch bowl. Stir in some of the brandy sauce from the apples, to taste.
5. Float the baked apples in the wassail. Garnish with orange slices. Serve hot in cups.

Note: To make a Baked Apple Ring Garnish, arrange 8 uncored, unpeeled small baking apples into a circle in a large baking dish. Secure each apple to the next with wooden toothpicks. Cover and bake as above.

To make the Rum Butter:
1. While the pudding is steaming, in the small bowl of an electric mixer beat the butter at medium speed until it is light and fluffy.
2. Gradually beat in the confectioners' sugar. Beat in the rum and vanilla until smooth. Cover and refrigerate.
3. Let the Rum Butter stand at room temperature for 30 minutes to soften before serving.
4. Loosen the edges of the pudding with a knife and unmold onto a serving plate. Serve warm with Rum Butter.

Note: Cooled pudding can be refrigerated or frozen, tightly wrapped in plastic wrap, then reheated. Thaw frozen pudding at room temperature before reheating. Bring refrigerated pudding to room temperature. To reheat, replace unwrapped pudding in the same clean, buttered mold. Cover tightly and steam as before for 45 minutes to 1 hour. Cool for 10 minutes. Unmold onto a serving plate.

FOOD AS GIFTS

T he pungent, sweet aromas of herbs, spices, citrus fruits, berries, and edible flowers will mingle deliciously in your kitchen as you create these homemade gifts for friends and family. The following pages are filled with ideas for condiments and preserves that serve as delightful tokens of the season. Stock up on pretty jars and ceramic crocks, bright ribbons for making bows, and perhaps some woven baskets in which you can pack the filled jars and containers nestled in crinkly red and green tissue paper.

LEMON DILL MUSTARD

Because mayonnaise is mixed into this savory mustard, it is not a mixture that keeps for very long. Make some to give to friends as a housewarming or drop-off gift. They will surely appreciate it during these hectic days, whether they are entertaining or simply Christmas shopping and tending a busy family. The mustard does equally well set on the buffet table to accompany ham or smoked salmon, or served at less formal suppers to dress up broiled fish and baked potatoes.

Makes 1½ cups

1 cup Dijon mustard
¼ cup light corn syrup
2 tablespoons chopped fresh parsley
2 tablespoons chopped fresh dill or
*   1 teaspoon dried dillweed*
2 teaspoons freshly squeezed lemon juice
2 teaspoons finely grated lemon zest
½ cup mayonnaise

1.   In a small bowl, whisk together the mustard, corn syrup, parsley, dill, lemon juice, and lemon zest. Mix well.

2.   Whisk in the mayonnaise.

3.   Spoon into glass or ceramic containers, cover, and refrigerate. The mustard will keep for 5 to 6 days.

CITRUS MUSTARD

In the early days of the century, before refrigeration and modern shipping methods, oranges were treasured fruits at Christmastime. Here, a touch of orange adds mellow tang to honey-laced mustard, which is further emboldened by lemon and lemon thyme. The flavors combine to make this one of the best mustards to serve with ham or poultry. Give this to anyone on your list who loves making elaborate sandwiches or mixing mustard into vinaigrettes—smashing used either way.

3. Spoon into glass or ceramic containers, cover, and refrigerate. The mustard will keep for 3 to 4 days.

HERBES DE PROVENCE

This mixture of dried herbs will keep for several months. Add a pinch or two to stews and soups, and to mustards and other sauces.

Makes ¾ cup

3 tablespoons dried marjoram
3 tablespoons dried thyme
3 tablespoons dried summer savory
1 tablespoon dried basil
1½ tablespoons dried rosemary
½ teaspoon dried or rubbed sage
½ teaspoon fennel seed
¼ teaspoon dried lavender

In a small bowl, mix together all the ingredients. Store in a glass container in a cool, dry, dark place.

Makes 1½ cups

1 cup Dijon mustard
½ cup honey
2 tablespoons freshly squeezed orange juice
1 tablespoon finely grated orange zest
2 teaspoons freshly squeezed lemon juice
1 teaspoon dried lemon thyme or 1 tablespoon chopped fresh lemon thyme

1. In a small bowl, whisk together the mustard, honey, orange juice, orange zest, lemon juice, and lemon thyme until blended.
2. Spoon into glass or ceramic containers, cover, and refrigerate. The mustard will keep for up to 2 weeks.

HERBED MUSTARD PROVENÇAL

Dried herbs are used to their best advantage in this recipe for sour cream-enriched mustard. As with the Lemon Dill Mustard (see page 104), this will not keep for too long and is meant as an offering that will be opened and used soon after giving. It is especially good with cold lamb and beef. Or, a tablespoon of honey stirred in the mustard transforms it into a tasty coating for a leg of lamb destined for roasting. Include a handsome hand-printed card explaining its many uses when you give this mustard.

Makes 1½ cups

1 heaping tablespoon Herbes de Provence
1½ tablespoons dry white wine
¾ cup Dijon mustard
¾ cup sour cream

1. In a cup, soak the Herbes de Provence in the wine for a few minutes to soften.
2. In a small bowl, whisk together the mustard and the sour cream. Gradually whisk in the herb mixture.

Storing and Using Dried Herbs

All dried herbs do best stored in glass or small plastic containers with tight-fitting lids and kept in a cool, dark cupboard. Just before using, rub them with your fingertips in the palm of your hand. The friction and the heat of your hand will release the natural oils in the leaves and bring out their flavor.

HONEY THYME MUSTARD

. . . .

The mustard seed and vinegar give this offering bite that is nicely muted by the honey, while corn-starch thickens it to a spreadable consistency. Serve the mustard with ham, pork, or hard, mellow cheeses.

Makes 2⅓ cups

⅓ cup dry white wine
¼ cup dry mustard
2 tablespoons mustard seed
½ cup honey
¼ cup white wine vinegar
¼ teaspoon salt
3 tablespoons cornstarch
1 cup cold water
1 teaspoon dried thyme or 1 tablespoon
  chopped fresh thyme

1. In a blender or food processor, combine the wine, mustard, and mustard seed, and process to a coarse puree, scraping down the sides occasionally. Cover and let stand at room temperature overnight to allow the flavors to develop.
2. Add the honey, vinegar, and salt. Process until blended.
3. In a small saucepan, stir the cornstarch with a little of the water to make a smooth paste. Whisk in the remaining water and the mustard mixture. Whisk over medium heat until thickened and bubbly.
4. Whisk in the thyme. Let the mustard cool, then spoon into glass or ceramic containers, cover, and refrigerate. The mustard will keep for up to 2 weeks.

TARRAGON MUSTARD

. . . .

For the best taste, let this mustard mellow in the refrigerator for a day or two to give the tarragon flavor time to develop. Serve the mustard with chicken, veal, vegetables, and cold seafood.

Makes 1½ cups

⅔ cup white wine vinegar or tarragon
  vinegar
½ cup dry mustard
1 cup packed light brown sugar
¼ teaspoon salt
½ cup olive oil
2 tablespoons chopped fresh tarragon or
  2 teaspoons dried tarragon

1. In a small bowl, combine the vinegar and the mustard. Stir and let stand for 15 minutes.
2. Put the mustard mixture in a food processor or blender. Add the brown sugar and salt and process until smooth. With the machine still running, add the olive oil in a slow, thin stream. The mustard should have the consistency of mayonnaise.
3. Stir in the tarragon, then spoon the mustard into glass or ceramic containers, cover, and refrigerate. The mustard will keep for up to 2 weeks.

ORANGE MINT MUSTARD

. . . .

The taste of fresh orange is a luscious surprise in mustard, and the addition of mint accentuates the fla-

vor even more. Serve this with ham, pork, or chicken, or slather it on a variety of sandwiches.

Makes 1 cup

1 cup Dijon mustard
1 tablespoon freshly squeezed orange juice
1 tablespoon grated orange zest
1 tablespoon finely chopped fresh mint

1. In a small bowl, combine all the ingredients. Mix well and let stand, covered, at room temperature overnight to blend the flavors.
2. Spoon into glass or ceramic containers, cover, and refrigerate. The mustard will keep for up to 2 weeks.

RASPBERRY VINAIGRETTE

. . . .

What a nice idea! Present a busy friend with this tasty vinaigrette in a pretty bottle. You might suggest she remove the garlic clove after a day or two so that it does not overwhelm the vinaigrette.

Makes ¾ cup

½ cup extra virgin olive oil
¼ cup raspberry vinegar
½ to 1 whole clove garlic
½ teaspoon Dijon mustard
½ teaspoon salt

In a screwtop jar, combine the olive oil, raspberry vinegar, garlic, mustard, and salt. Cover and shake until blended. Store in the refrigerator for up to a week. Remove the garlic clove before serving.

TOMATO LEMON CHUTNEY

Made with chili pepper, tomatoes, and a good measure of sugar and raisins, this condiment is a glorious mixture of sweet and piquant taste sensations.

Makes 2⅓ cups

1 tablespoon vegetable oil
1 whole fresh chili pepper, chopped, or 1 dried chili pepper, crumbled
½ teaspoon cumin seed
¼ teaspoon mustard seed
¼ teaspoon ground nutmeg
1½ pounds tomatoes, cored and very thinly sliced
½ lemon, halved and seeded
½ cup sugar
⅓ cup raisins or dried currants

1. Heat the oil in a large, heavy saucepan over medium-high heat. Add the chili pepper, cumin seed, mustard seed, and nutmeg. When the seeds start to jump in the pan, add the tomatoes. Lay the lemon quarters on top, cut sides down.
2. Lower the heat, cover, and simmer very gently for 15 minutes, stirring occasionally to prevent sticking.
3. Stir in the sugar and raisins and bring to a boil. Lower the heat and simmer gently, uncovered, for 25 to 35 minutes or until thickened, stirring often.
4. Remove the lemon quarters. Let the chutney cool to room temperature. Spoon into glass or ceramic containers, cover, and refrigerate. The chutney will keep for up to a week.

CRANBERRY CHUTNEY

This colorful chutney bursts with fresh fruit flavor without being too sweet and as such is delicious served with game birds and poultry. Leftovers will keep for a week or so in the refrigerator.

Makes 4 cups

4 cups fresh cranberries (1 pound)
2 Granny Smith apples, peeled, cored, and chopped
1 pear, peeled, cored, and chopped
1 cup golden raisins
1 cup minced onion
1 cup sugar
1 tablespoon grated orange zest
1 teaspoon ground cinnamon
⅛ teaspoon freshly grated nutmeg
½ cup freshly squeezed orange juice
2 tablespoons Cointreau, Grand Marnier, or other orange-flavored liqueur
2 tablespoons cognac

1. In a heavy, 3-quart saucepan, combine the cranberries, apples, pear, raisins, onion, sugar, orange zest, cinnamon, and nutmeg. Stir in the orange juice.
2. Bring the mixture to a boil over high heat. Reduce the heat and simmer, uncovered, for about 45 minutes or until thickened, stirring occasionally.
3. Stir in the orange-flavored liqueur and cognac. Let the chutney cool to room temperature. Ladle into glass or ceramic containers, cover, and refrigerate.

MINTED CHUTNEY

Fruity chutney flavored with fresh mint is a welcome change from other condiments. If short of time, buy a good commercial chutney and stir chopped fresh mint into it.

Makes 3 ¾ cups

1 cup cider vinegar
1 cup sugar
3 cups chopped red bell peppers
2 cups pitted, coarsely chopped apricots, peaches, or apples
1½ cups seeded, chopped, unpeeled orange
1 cup chopped onion
⅓ cup golden raisins
⅓ cup chopped crystallized ginger (about 2 ounces)
1 clove garlic, minced
½ teaspoon salt
⅓ cup chopped raw cashews
2 tablespoons chopped fresh mint

1. In a heavy, 4-quart saucepan, stir together ¾ cup of the vinegar and sugar. Bring to a boil over medium heat and cook, uncovered, for 5 minutes, stirring occasionally.
2. Stir in the peppers, apricots, orange, onion, raisins, ginger, garlic, and salt. Bring the mixture back to a boil, stirring constantly. Lower the heat and simmer for 30 minutes, stirring often.
3. Stir in the cashews and the remaining ¼ cup vinegar. Cook for 20 to 30 minutes or until the mixture has thickened, stirring often.
4. Stir in the mint. Let the chutney cool to room temperature. Ladle into glass or ceramic containers, cover, and refrigerate for up to 2 weeks.

LEMON RELISH

Because this relish is meant to have a chunky consistency, chop the vegetables with a knife, not in the food processor. Serve with broiled or grilled fish.

Makes 3½ cups

1¼ cups peeled, seeded, chopped ripe tomatoes
1 cup peeled, seeded, chopped cucumber
¾ cup uncooked sweet corn kernels, cut from the cob (1 to 2 medium ears), or slightly thawed frozen corn kernels
⅔ cup chopped red onion
⅓ cup chopped yellow bell pepper
⅓ cup chopped red bell pepper
3 tablespoons chopped scallions (including green parts)
3 tablespoons sugar
1 teaspoon salt
1 teaspoon celery seed
⅛ teaspoon ground cinnamon
⅛ teaspoon ground nutmeg
⅛ teaspoon black pepper
Pinch of ground cloves
½ cup freshly squeezed lemon juice

1. In a large bowl, combine the tomatoes, cucumber, corn, onion, bell peppers, and scallions. Sprinkle with the sugar, salt, celery seed, cinnamon, nutmeg, black pepper, and cloves. Mix together well.
2. Drizzle the lemon juice over the mixture and stir to combine. Cover and let the mixture stand at room temperature for 1 to 4 hours.
3. Drain the vegetable mixture in a colander, saving the juices. Return the vegetable mixture to the same bowl. Put the juices in a small saucepan and bring to a boil over medium-high heat. Continue to boil until the liquid has reduced by half. Stir the hot juices back into the vegetable mixture.
4. Let the relish cool to room temperature. Ladle into glass or ceramic containers, cover, and refrigerate. The relish will keep for up to a week.

Gift Tags and Labels

While you can buy holiday cards that are perfect for attaching to a jar or bottle of jam or vinaigrette, making your own adds a particularly personal touch. Buy fine-textured writing paper, cut or fold it into a workable size, then print your holiday message on it using your best script. With many of these gifts, you might also want to include serving suggestions. Thread a narrow ribbon through a hole punched into the tag and tie it around the top of the jar or bottle. Alternatively, self-sticking labels, decorated or plain, can turn a jar of homemade chutney or marmalade into a very intimate gift.

STRAWBERRY RHUBARB CONSERVE

This sweet, chunky conserve is a mixture as at home on the breakfast buffet or tea table as it is on the dessert tray. Serve with griddle cakes or hot scones, or use to dress up a scoop of ice cream crowning a slice of pound cake.

Makes 2½ pints

4 cups fresh strawberries, hulled and
*   halved or quartered if large (about*
*   1¼ pounds)*
3½ cups cut fresh rhubarb, cut in
*   ½-inch pieces (about 1 pound)*
½ cup cold water
½ cup fruit wine such as elderberry,
*   dessert wine such as sweet Marsala,*
*   or sweet red wine*
⅓ cup dried currants
2 cinnamon sticks
5 cups sugar
½ cup chopped almonds
½ cup chopped walnuts

1. In a heavy, 6- to 8-quart non-reactive (enamel or stainless steel) saucepan, combine the strawberries, rhubarb, water, fruit wine, currants, and cinnamon sticks. Stir in the sugar and mix well.

2. Bring the mixture to a boil over high heat, stirring constantly with a long-handled wooden spoon. Continue to boil until the mixture is very thick and sheets off a metal spoon, stirring constantly. Add the nuts during the last 5 minutes of cooking.

3. Remove the pan from the heat. Skim off the foam from the top and stir gently. Remove the cinnamon sticks with a slotted spoon.

4. Quickly ladle the conserve into 5 hot, sterilized ½-pint glass canning jars, leaving a ¼-inch headspace. Seal with canning lids according to the manufacturer's directions.

5. Process the sealed hot conserve in a boiling water bath for 5 minutes after the water returns to a full boil. (Add 1 minute processing time for each 1,000 feet above sea level.) Cool the conserve upright on a rack. Store in a cool, dry, dark place.

ROSE PETAL JAM

Syrupy Rose Petal Jam is meant to be served with freshly baked scones and biscuits before a warm fire on a cold afternoon. It brings the delicate fragrance of springtime to the winter tea table as few other foods do.

Makes 1¼ cups

1½ cups lightly packed pesticide-free rose
*   petals (about 6 large rose blossoms)*
1½ cups cold water
1⅓ cups sugar
¼ cup freshly squeezed lemon juice
1 teaspoon rose water (optional)

1. Wash the rose petals and spread them out on paper towels to dry. Snip out the bitter white heels and any brown spots.

2. In a heavy large nonreactive (enamel or stainless steel) saucepan, combine the rose petals and water. Stir in the sugar, lemon juice and, if roses were not very fragrant, the rose water. Bring the mixture to a rolling boil over medium-high heat, stirring constantly with a wooden spoon.

3. Lower the heat to medium. Continue to boil for 25 to 30 minutes or until the mixture has thickened, stirring often. A spoonful of jam should hold its shape on a cold plate.

4. Remove the jam from the heat. Skim off any foam from the top.

5. Quickly ladle the jam into 2 hot, sterilized, 6-ounce glass jars, leaving a ¼-inch headspace. Seal the tops with melted paraffin. When cool, cover the jars with lids. Store in a cool, dark place for up to 2 weeks.

THREE-FRUIT MARMALADE

In the nursery rhyme, the queen suggested marmalade for bread. We think it tastes delicious on muffins and biscuits, too, either at breakfast or teatime. Making the marmalade with three different citrus fruits turns an ordinary spread into one worthy of being presented as a princely gift.

Makes 3 pints

1½ pounds mixed citrus fruits (grapefruit, oranges, and lemons), washed, dried, quartered, and seeded but not peeled
12 cups cold water
6 cups sugar

1. Cut the fruit quarters into very thin slices, working over a bowl to catch the juices.
2. Measure 4 cups of the fruit slices, including juices, into a heavy, 8-quart nonreactive (enamel or stainless steel) saucepan. Add the water. Cover and let stand for 24 hours.
3. Bring the mixture to a boil over high heat. Remove the lid, lower the heat to medium, and boil gently for 2 to 2½ hours or until reduced to 6 cups, stirring often. Cool slightly.
4. Add the sugar. Bring to a boil over high heat, stirring constantly with a long-handled wooden spoon to dissolve the sugar. Keep the mixture at a rapid boil until it sheets off a metal spoon and registers 220°F. on a candy thermometer.
5. Remove the pan from the heat.

Skim off the foam from the top and stir gently.

6. Quickly ladle the marmalade into 6 hot, sterilized ½-pint glass canning jars, leaving a ¼-inch headspace. Seal with canning lids according to the manufacturer's directions.

7. Process the sealed hot marmalade in a boiling water bath for 5 minutes after the water returns to a full boil. (Add 1 minute processing time for each 1,000 feet above sea level.) Cool upright on a rack and store in a cool, dry, dark place.

The Language of Flowers

The language of flowers, so cherished by the Victorians, invaded nearly every aspect of domestic life. Roses, violets, lavender, and rose geraniums were grown in most Victorian gardens, prized as much for their fragrance as for their appearance. The dried petals and leaves often found their way into potpourris and sachets, although just as often they were spirited away to the kitchen, where their fragile scent gently perfumed jams and jellies.

LAVENDER JELLY

Lavender Jelly is one of the prettiest homemade Christmas presents you can give. A shining jar nestled in a gift basket turns a simple gesture into a thoughtful offering.

Makes 2 pints

Lavender Infusion:
3 tablespoons dried lavender, or ½ cup lightly packed, pesticide-free fresh lavender
3 cups distilled water

Jelly:
4 cups sugar
¼ cup cider vinegar
1 (3 ounce) package liquid fruit pectin
Blue food coloring (optional)
Fresh lavender sprigs, for garnish (optional)

To make the Lavender Infusion:

1. Put the lavender flowers in a medium bowl. Bring the distilled water to a boil in a nonreactive (enamel or stainless steel) saucepan and pour the water over the flowers.

2. Cover the bowl and let stand for 15 minutes. Strain the infusion through a sieve lined with damp cheesecloth. Discard the lavender.

To make the Jelly:

1. Measure 2 cups of the Lavender Infusion into a heavy, 6-quart non-reactive (enamel or stainless steel) saucepan. Stir in the sugar and vinegar and mix well. Bring to a full boil over high heat, stirring constantly with a long-handled wooden spoon.

2. Stir in the liquid pectin. The vinegar and liquid pectin will turn the color of the infusion to magenta. Bring to a high rolling boil that cannot be stirred down. Continue to boil for precisely 1 minute, stirring constantly.

3. Remove the pan from the heat. For a lavender color, stir in a few drops of blue food coloring. Skim off the foam from the top.

4. Quickly ladle the jelly into 4 hot, sterilized ½-pint glass canning jars, leaving a ¼-inch headspace. If you choose not to garnish the jelly, seal with canning lids according to the manufacturer's directions. Cool the jelly upright on a rack. Store in the refrigerator for up to 1 month.

5. To garnish the jelly with lavender sprigs, do not seal the jars immediately. Tent them very loosely with plastic wrap and cool on a rack for 5 hours. Using a narrow spatula, gently press lavender sprigs into the surface of the jelly. Seal the jars and let them stand for 24 hours. Store in the refrigerator for up to 1 month.

6. For longer storage, process the sealed hot jelly in a boiling water bath for 5 minutes after the water returns to a full boil. (Add 1 minute processing time for each 1,000 feet above sea level.) Cool on a rack and store in a cool, dry, dark place.

Note: Use distilled water for the Lavender Infusion to avoid chemicals in tap water that may alter the color.

COOKIES AND CANDIES

I n countless households, the weeks before the holiday bear witness to happy activity in the kitchen, as tray upon tray of cookies is pulled from the oven, cooled on crowded counters, then enjoyed by family and guests alike. It is also the time of year when we attempt candy making, a task that in reality is no more difficult than baking.

A tin of homemade cookies or candies makes a cherished gift. During the weeks before Thanksgiving, buy colorful and decorative tins and boxes in anticipation of the festive treats with which they will be filled.

PUMPKIN MADELEINES

These boldly flavored miniature cakelike cookies are probably not what Marcel Proust had in mind, but had he tasted their rich pumpkin flavor so in keeping with the season, surely he would have rhapsodized about these madeleines.

Makes about 20 cookies

2 large eggs
⅔ cup sugar
8 tablespoons (1 stick) unsalted butter, melted
1 cup plus 1 tablespoon all-purpose flour
2 tablespoons unsweetened pumpkin pulp (canned or fresh, cooked, and mashed)
1 teaspoon freshly squeezed lemon juice
¼ teaspoon pumpkin pie spice
Dash of salt

1. In the medium bowl of an electric mixer, beat the eggs and sugar at high speed for about 5 minutes or until light and fluffy.

2. Meanwhile, pour 2 tablespoons of the melted butter into a small bowl. Blend in 1 tablespoon of the flour. Brush 2 madeleine molds with this mixture to prevent sticking.

3. Beat the remaining 1 cup flour into the egg mixture at low speed. Gradually beat in the remaining 6 tablespoons butter.

4. Increase the speed to medium and beat in the pumpkin pulp, lemon juice, pumpkin pie spice, and salt until well blended. Cover and let the mixture stand at room temperature for 1 hour.

5. Preheat the oven to 375°F.

6. Spoon the batter into the prepared madeleine molds, using about 1½ tablespoons for each cookie. Do not spread the batter in the molds. Bake for 15 to 20 minutes or until golden brown.

7. Remove the madeleines from the molds at once and cool on a rack. They are best eaten within a few hours of baking. Or, wrap airtight and freeze for up to 8 weeks.

Note: Madeleine molds are available at gourmet kitchen stores.

LEMON VERBENA LACE COOKIES
....

If you cannot find shiny-leaved lemon verbena, it's all right to omit it from the recipe. The lemon flavor will not be as pronounced, but the cookies will work just as well.

Makes about 14 cookies

½ cup sugar
3 tablespoons all-purpose flour
Pinch of salt
1⅓ cups sliced almonds
2 large egg whites
2 tablespoons (¼ stick) unsalted butter, melted and cooled slightly
1 tablespoon minced fresh lemon verbena
2 teaspoons grated lemon zest
¼ teaspoon vanilla extract
⅛ teaspoon almond extract
⅛ teaspoon lemon extract
3 ounces semisweet chocolate, coarsely chopped

1.   In a medium bowl, blend the sugar, flour, and salt. Add the almonds and toss to coat. Stir in the egg whites, butter, lemon verbena, lemon zest, and the vanilla, almond, and lemon extracts. Mix together well. Cover and refrigerate overnight.

2.   Preheat the oven to 350°F. Lightly butter a baking sheet. Spread 1 tablespoon of batter into a 3-inch circle on the baking sheet. Repeat with the remaining batter, spacing the cookies 3 inches apart, making only 4 cookies at one time. Bake for 8 to 10 minutes or until lightly browned around the edges.

3.   Working quickly, loosen the hot cookies from the sheet and imme-diately curve them over a rolling pin or small inverted bowl. Set aside to cool on a rack.

4.   Repeat with the remaining but-ter, lightly buttering the baking sheet each time.

5.   In the top of a double boiler over hot, not simmering, water, melt the chocolate, stirring constantly. Re-move from the heat.

6.   Dip the edges of the cooled cookies in the melted chocolate. Put the chocolate-trimmed cookies on waxed paper until the chocolate sets.

LEMON TRIANGLES
....

What a nice change these lemon bars are from brownies and blondies, the usual bar cookies one finds on des-sert tables and tea trays. These are tangy-sweet and refreshing all at once, a sensation provided by the good measure of fresh lemon juice that flavors the moist filling.

Makes 24 large cookies or
48 teatime cookies

Crust:
2½ cups all-purpose flour
1 cup (2 sticks) unsalted butter, chilled and cut into small pieces
⅔ cup confectioners' sugar
¼ cup (½ stick) margarine, chilled and cut into small pieces

Filling:
½ cup all-purpose flour
¾ teaspoon baking soda
5 large eggs
2½ cups granulated sugar
6 tablespoons freshly squeezed lemon juice
Confectioners' sugar, for garnish

To make the Crust:

1.   Preheat the oven to 350°F.

2.   In the large bowl of an electric mixer, combine the flour, butter, con-fectioners' sugar, and margarine. Beat at low speed for about 1 minute. In-crease the speed to medium and con-tinue to beat until the mixture is crumbly.

3.   Press the dough into an un-greased 15½ × 10½ × 1-inch jelly-roll pan. Bake for 15 to 20 minutes or until crust is firm to the touch but not brown. Do not turn off the oven.

To make the Filling:

1.   In a small bowl, sift together the flour and the baking soda.

2.   In a medium mixing bowl, beat the eggs, granulated sugar, and lemon juice at medium speed until light. Re-duce the speed to low. Add the flour mixture and beat just until blended. Pour the mixture over the hot baked crust. The pan will be very full.

3.   Bake in the 350°F. oven for 25 minutes or until the filling is set, lightly browned, and pulls away from the edges of the pan.

4.   Let cool completely in the pan on a rack. Sprinkle with confectioners' sugar. Cut into 5-inch squares. Cut each square in half diagonally in both directions, making 4 triangles. For teatime cookies, cut each triangle in half again.

LEMON COOKIES WITH GINGER MARMALADE

A bit of ginger marmalade is folded into clouds of whipped cream, then sandwiched between buttery lemon cookies, for a delectable treat indeed. They can be made well ahead of time and refrigerated; however, they should be served or presented as a gift on the day they are filled.

Makes 48 cookies, 24 sandwich cookies

Lemon Cookies:
1 cup sugar
½ cup (1 stick) unsalted butter, softened
½ teaspoon vanilla extract
¼ to ½ teaspoon lemon extract
Grated zest of 1 lemon
1 large egg
1½ cups cake flour
¼ teaspoon cream of tartar

Ginger Filling:
½ cup ginger marmalade, plus a little
  extra for garnish
½ cup heavy cream, whipped

To make the Lemon Cookies:
1.   In the medium bowl of an electric mixer, beat together the sugar, butter, the vanilla and the lemon extracts, and the lemon zest for 4 to 5 minutes at medium speed until fluffy. Beat in the egg.
2.   In a small bowl sift together the flour and cream of tartar. Gradually beat the flour mixture into the butter mixture at low speed.
3.   Divide the dough in half. Shape each half in a log 1½ inches in diameter. Wrap each log in plastic wrap and refrigerate for several hours or overnight.
4.   Preheat the oven to 400°F. Using a sharp knife, cut each cookie dough log in 24 thin slices. Put the slices on ungreased baking sheets ½ inch apart. Bake for 7 to 8 minutes, until the edges are lightly browned. Remove the cookies from the baking sheets and cool completely on racks.

To make the Ginger Filling:
1.   In a medium bowl, fold the ½ cup ginger marmalade into the whipped cream.
2.   Turn half the cooled cookies bottom side up. Spoon about 1 tablespoon of the filling onto each of these cookies. Top with the remaining cookies. Garnish each with a dab of ginger marmalade.

MARITIME GINGERSNAPS

These little round cookies are flavored with ginger, cinnamon, and cloves, all spices we readily associate with the winter holidays. These make a wonderful gift packed into colorful tins.

Makes 48 cookies

½ cup molasses
¼ cup solid vegetable shortening
1½ cups all-purpose flour
2 teaspoons ground ginger
1 teaspoon ground cinnamon
1 teaspoon ground cloves
¼ teaspoon baking powder
¼ teaspoon salt

1.   In a small saucepan, combine the molasses and shortening and stir over medium heat until boiling. Immediately remove the mixture from the heat and let cool to room temperature, about 30 minutes.
2.   In a large mixing bowl, place the flour, ginger, cinnamon, cloves, baking powder, and salt. Stir until well blended.
3.   Pour the cooled molasses mixture over the flour mixture and mix together well to form a dough. Chill the dough in the refrigerator for about 10 minutes.
4.   Preheat the oven to 375°F.
5.   Divide the dough in quarters. Cut each quarter in 12 equal pieces. Shape each piece of dough into a very small (½-inch) ball. Put the balls of dough on ungreased baking sheets, 2 inches apart.
6.   Flatten the balls of dough with the bottom of a small glass or with your palm to make them about the size of a quarter. Bake for 6 to 8 minutes or until crisp and dry.
7.   Remove the gingersnaps from the oven and cool them on racks, still on the baking sheets, for 5 minutes. Remove them from the baking sheets with a metal spatula and cool completely on racks.

HEART COOKIES

With one simple recipe and two different heart-shaped cutters you can assemble a plateful of graceful cookies—some filled with bright red jam, others dusted with snowy confectioners' sugar.

Makes about 24 sandwich cookies, 24 small heart cookies

2 cups all-purpose flour
½ cup confectioners' sugar
¼ teaspoon salt
1 cup (2 sticks) unsalted butter, cut into
    small pieces and softened
¼ cup raspberry jam
Confectioners' sugar, for garnish

1. In a food processor, combine the flour, the ½ cup confectioners' sugar, and salt. Process until blended.
2. Add the butter and pulse until the mixture resembles coarse meal. Continue to process until the dough pulls away from the bowl and forms a ball. Wrap the dough in plastic wrap and refrigerate for 1 hour.
3. Preheat the oven to 325°F.
4. On a well-floured work surface, roll out half the dough to a thickness of ⅛ inch. Return the remaining dough to the refrigerator until ready to roll it. Using a 2½-inch heart-shaped cutter, cut the dough into heart shapes. Put the hearts on an ungreased baking sheet 1 inch apart. (Gather the trimmings and add them to the remaining dough in the refrigerator., using a 1-inch heart-shaped cutter, cut out the centers from half these cookies. Put both the cut-out hearts

and the small heart centers on another ungreased baking sheet.
5. Bake the cookies until lightly browned, about 14 to 16 minutes for the large solid hearts, 10 to 12 minutes for the cut-out hearts and the small hearts. Use visual tests for doneness as well as time.
6. Let the cookies cool on the baking sheets for a few minutes. Using a metal spatula, carefully transfer the cookies to racks to cool completely.

7. Repeat the process with the remaining dough.

To assemble:
1. When the cookies are cool, spread the bottom side of each large solid heart with ½ teaspoon of raspberry jam. Sift confectioners' sugar over the tops of the cut-out hearts and place on the jam-topped hearts. Sift confectioners' sugar over the small heart cookies.

LAVENDER SHORTBREAD FINGERS

Sprinkled with little lavender flowers, these iced-cookie strips are stunning on a dessert plate. Bring them as a gift—they are always welcomed by busy hostesses, particularly during the holidays.

Makes 16 cookies

Shortbread:
2 cups (4 sticks) unsalted butter, slightly softened
1 cup superfine sugar or confectioners' sugar
3 cups sifted all-purpose flour
1 cup rice flour

Lavender Icing:
3½ to 4 cups confectioners' sugar
⅓ cup Lavender Infusion (see page 109)
Fresh lavender, for garnish

To make the Shortbread:
1.   In the large bowl of an electric mixer, beat the butter at medium speed. Gradually add the sugar, beating until just blended. Do not overbeat or the butter will become oily.
2.   Using a wooden spoon or pastry blender, quickly work in the flours, handling the dough as little as possible.
3.   Divide the dough in half. Lightly dust a work surface with a mixture of half flour, half confectioners' sugar. Lightly flour your hands with the mixture.
4.   Pat each piece of dough into an 8 × 5-inch rectangle, ¾ inch thick. Using the tines of a fork, prick the dough crosswise in straight lines to mark 8 (1-inch) strips, and then lengthwise in half, to form 16 fingers. The tines should almost go through the dough.
5.   Prick the dough lightly all over with the tines of a fork, to prevent puffing. Using 2 spatulas, transfer the shortbread fingers to an ungreased baking sheet 1 inch apart. Cover and freeze for 30 minutes.
6.   Preheat the oven to 375°F.
7.   Bake the shortbread for 5 minutes. Lower the oven temperature to 300°F. Continue baking the shortbread for 45 minutes to 1 hour or until it just begins to turn light brown around the edges.
8.   Cool the shortbread on racks, still on the baking sheet, for 15 minutes. Using a thin, sharp knife, carefully cut the warm shortbread into fingers along the pricked lines. Set the fingers on racks, 1 inch apart, to cool completely.

To make the Lavender Icing:
1.   In a medium bowl, gradually sift enough confectioners' sugar into the Lavender Infusion to make a thick but pourable icing, whisking until smooth after each addition.
2.   Put a sheet of waxed paper under the cooling racks holding the shortbread fingers. Drizzle the icing over the fingers, letting it drip down the sides. Sprinkle immediately with fresh lavender flowers. Let the shortbread stand until the icing sets.

CHOCOLATE MINT SHORTBREAD COOKIES

Pack this shortbread in tins decorated with a tartan pattern. The frosting could not be easier to make—the sweet mint patties melt into a seductive icing for the wonderfully buttery cookies.

Makes about 24 to 36 cookies

1 (7½-ounce) package chocolate-covered mint patties
1 (7½-ounce) package shortbread cookies
1 to 2 teaspoons milk (optional)

1.   Put the patties in the top of a double boiler over barely simmering water and stir until melted and smooth. Remove from the heat. If the frosting is too thick to spread, stir in 1 to 2 teaspoons milk.
2.   Frost the shortbread cookies with the melted patties. Let the cookies stand on waxed paper until the frosting sets.

Mailing Cookies

Pack cookies and candies in airtight tins with plenty of waxed or tissue paper to keep them from jostling about. Set the tins in a larger box and surround them with shredded or crumbled newspaper, foam pellets, or popcorn. Wrap the box in brown paper and write "fragile" on it in large letters. Make sure you send the package first class.

RICH MAN'S SHORTBREAD

. . . .

Shortbread is a humble cookie, proving that the simplest things in life are often the best. But it is possible to improve upon perfection, as evidenced here when rich toffee is spread on top of the baked shortbread, then covered with a thin shell of chocolate.

Makes 24 cookies

Shortbread:
½ cup (1 stick) unsalted butter, softened
4½ tablespooons superfine sugar
1⅓ cups all-purpose flour

Toffee Topping:
⅔ cup (half of a 14-ounce can)
*   sweetened condensed milk (not*
*   evaporated milk)*
½ cup (1 stick) unsalted butter
4½ tablespoons superfine sugar
2 tablespoons corn syrup
¼ teaspoon vanilla extract

Chocolate Glaze:
7 ounces semisweet chocolate, coarsely
*   chopped*

To make the Shortbread:
1.   Preheat the oven to 350°F.
2.   In the large bowl of an electric mixer, cream the butter and sugar at medium speed for 4 to 5 minutes or until light and fluffy.
3.   Stir in the flour with a wooden spoon. When well combined, press the mixture into an ungreased 10 × 6 × 1½-inch baking pan. Bake for 20 to 25 minutes or until it is golden brown.
4.   Cool in the pan on a rack.

To make the Toffee Topping:
1.   In a heavy, medium saucepan, combine the condensed milk, butter, sugar, and corn syrup. Bring to a boil over medium-high heat, then boil for about 5 minutes, stirring constantly with a long-handled wooden spoon.
2.   Stir in the vanilla. Quickly pour the toffee mixture over the cooled shortbread and spread it evenly with a metal spatula or kitchen knife. Let the topping cool for at least 1 hour.

To make the Chocolate Glaze:
1.   In the top of a double boiler over hot, not simmering, water, melt the chocolate, stirring until smooth.
2.   Pour the melted chocolate over the cooled topping, spreading it evenly with a metal spatula or kitchen knife.
3.   Let the glaze cool for several hours or until set. Cut the shortbread into 24 bars.

ENGLISH TOFFEE

. . . .

Packed into a small tin lined with tissue paper or plastic wrap, toffee makes an irresistible gift for anyone on your list with a sweet tooth. The melt-in-your-mouth candies are hard to ignore.

Makes 2 pounds

2½ cups sugar
1 cup (2 sticks) unsalted butter
1½ cups slivered almonds
1 teaspoon vanilla extract
6 ounces semisweet chocolate, coarsely
*   chopped*
½ cup finely chopped walnuts

1.   Butter two 15½ × 10½ × 1-inch jelly-roll pans.
2.   In a heavy, large saucepan, combine the butter and sugar. Cover and cook for 5 minutes over low heat, gradually raising the heat to medium-high. Uncover the saucepan and bring the mixture to a boil. Remove the saucepan from the heat and add the almonds.
3.   Put a candy thermometer in the saucepan and return it to the medium-high heat. Cook the toffee until the thermometer registers 290°F., or soft-crack stage.
4.   Remove the saucepan from the heat. Add the vanilla and stir vigorously with a long-handled wooden spoon. Quickly pour the mixture into the prepared jelly-roll pans, spreading evenly with a metal spatula. Cool completely.
5.   In the top of a double boiler over hot, not simmering, water, melt the chocolate, stirring to make sure it is smooth. Spread the melted chocolate over the cooled and hardened toffee. Sprinkle with chopped walnuts and cool completely.
6.   Break the toffee into chunks and store in tightly covered containers in a cool place.

constantly with a long-handled wooden spoon, until a candy thermometer inserted in the mixture registers 255°F., or hard-ball stage.

3.   Gradually and carefully stir in the scalded cream, keeping the mixture at a gentle boil. Add the butter, rum, and vanilla. Return the mixture to 255°F., stirring often.

4.   Pour the mixture into the prepared pan. When the caramel is almost cool, cut it into 36 squares. Cool completely in the pan.

5.   Wrap the caramels in waxed paper and store in the refrigerator for up to 5 days. To freeze, wrap in freezer plastic wrap. Let refrigerated candy soften at room temperature for 1 hour before serving. Let frozen candy soften at room temperature for about 2 hours.

ORANGE TRUFFLES

Infusing a mixture of chocolate and butter with a good dose of orange-flavored liqueur turns ordinary chocolate into elegant truffles. For the best results, be sure to cook the chocolate mixture to 160°F.

Makes 24 truffles

1 cup (2 sticks) unsalted butter
1 pound semisweet chocolate, coarsely chopped
6 large egg yolks
1/3 cup Cointreau, Grand Marnier, or other orange-flavored liqueur
Pink roses, for garnish, or finely chopped nuts, shredded coconut, unsweetened cocoa powder, or chocolate shavings for coating

MILK AND HONEY CARAMELS

Like toffee, caramels appeal to everyone who likes the flavor of butterscotch. These are easy to make and will keep in the refrigerator for several days. (If left too long at room temperature, a little cream may separate from the candies and cause them to be unpleasantly sticky.) These are great for gift-giving because you can make them well ahead of time and freeze them for several weeks.

Makes 1¾ pounds (36 caramels)

1¼ cups honey
1 cup sugar
½ cup milk
¼ cup light corn syrup
2 cups heavy cream, scalded
1 tablespoon unsalted butter
1 tablespoon dark rum
½ teaspoon vanilla extract

1.   Butter an 8 × 8 × 2-inch pan.
2.   In a heavy deep 4-quart saucepan, combine the honey, sugar, milk, and corn syrup. Stir over medium-low heat until blended. Increase the heat to medium and cook, stirring

1. In the top of a double boiler over barely simmering water, melt the butter. Add the chocolate and stir until melted and smooth.

2. In a small bowl, whisk the egg yolks together. Stir a few spoonfuls of the hot chocolate mixture into the egg yolks. Stir the yolk mixture back into the chocolate mixture in the double boiler. Cook, stirring constantly, for about 4 minutes, or until a candy thermometer inserted in the mixture registers 160°F.

3. Immediately pour the chocolate mixture into a medium bowl and let cool to room temperature for about 1 hour, stirring occasionally.

4. Gradually whisk the liqueur into the chocolate mixture. Cover and refrigerate for 8 hours or overnight.

5. With cold hands, quickly roll heaping teaspoonfuls of the chocolate mixture into balls. The chocolate will be firm when scooped from the bowl, but softens quickly. Put the truffles in paper or foil candy cups and decorate with pink roses. Or, roll them in chopped nuts, coconut, cocoa powder, or chocolate shavings.

6. Put truffles in a tightly lidded tin or other airtight container. Refrigerate the truffles if keeping for more than 1 or 2 days.

CHAMPAGNE TRUFFLES

In recent years, Champagne truffles have become one of the most popular of all truffles. To make these elegant chocolates you will need Champagne liqueur, available at fine liquor stores, as well as the best-tasting semisweet chocolate you can find. The combination is sublime

Makes about 18 truffles

8 ounces semisweet chocolate, coarsely chopped
½ cup unsweetened cocoa powder
½ cup heavy cream
2 tablespoons (¼ stick) unsalted butter, cut into pieces
1 tablespoon Champagne liqueur
Confectioners' sugar, for coating

1. In a food processor, combine the chocolate with the cocoa and process until pulverized. Set aside.

2. In a small saucepan, stir the cream, butter, and liqueur over medium heat until hot but not boiling. Pour the liquid over the chocolate in the food processor and process until smooth.

3. Pour the chocolate mixture into a medium bowl. Let the mixture cool to room temperature for about 1 hour, stirring occasionally. Cover and refrigerate for 8 hours or overnight.

4. With cold hands, quickly roll rounded teaspoonfuls of the chocolate mixture into balls. Roll the truffles in confectioners' sugar to coat and set them in paper or foil candy cups.

5. Put truffles in a tightly lidded tin or other airtight container. Refrigerate the truffles if keeping for more than 1 or 2 days.

Truffles

Round, bite-sized chocolates made from a classic ganache mixture of chocolate, cream, and occasionally butter are widely known as truffles. Sometimes the ganache centers are dipped in tempered chocolate for a hard-shell coating; other times they are simply rolled in cocoa powder. Regardless of the method, all truffles are sinfully delicious and make welcome gifts during the holidays when filling the house with sweet treats is part of tradition.

To give truffles as presents, pack them in airtight tins. Lay tissue paper or waxed paper between the layers; choose white paper as colored tissue may bleed when it comes in contact with the rich truffles. Keep the tins in the refrigerator until you are ready to give them away. If possible, make and give them on the same day—fresh truffles are the best.

BAKED GOODS

Few baked goods are as satisfying and welcome as breads, muffins, and biscuits—particularly at Christmastime. Having a fresh coffee cake on hand encourages us to invite the neighbors in to admire the Christmas tree; buttery scones are the perfect ending to a day of shopping with a friend; and just-baked breads are a lovely addition to holiday parties. The following recipes surely will inspire you to get out the baking pans and begin making wonderful treats.

WHEATBERRY FRENCH BREAD

These long, free-form loaves are excellent choices for holiday parties, their flavor and texture making them ideal for setting on the buffet table with strong cheeses, sliced ham, chutneys, and mustards. Because they have no fat, the loaves will not keep more than a day, so plan to serve them soon after you bake them.

Makes 2 loaves

5½ to 6½ cups all-purpose flour
3 packages (0.6 ounce each) refrigerated cake yeast, crumbled
2 teaspoons sugar
2 ½ cups lukewarm water (80° to 95°F.)
1 tablespoon salt
1 cup cracked wheat
½ cup whole-wheat flour

1. In the large bowl of an electric mixer, combine 2½ cups of the all-purpose flour with the yeast and sugar. Mix together well. Stir in the lukewarm water. Let stand for 20 minutes.

2. Beat at medium speed for 2 minutes. Add 1 cup of the all-purpose flour and the salt. Beat at low speed for 20 seconds. Beat at high speed for 2 minutes.

3. Stir in the cracked wheat and whole-wheat flour with a wooden spoon. Gradually stir in up to 2 cups more of the all-purpose flour to make a moderately stiff dough.

4. Turn the dough out onto a floured surface. Knead for 10 to 15 minutes or until the dough is smooth and no longer sticky, adding enough of the remaining 1 cup all-purpose flour if necessary to prevent sticking.

5. Put the dough in a large greased bowl. Lightly grease the surface of the dough. Cover with plastic wrap and refrigerate overnight.

6. Butter a baking sheet. Punch down the dough and divide it in half. On a floured surface, roll or pat each half into a 12 × 8-inch rectangle. Roll up each piece of dough, starting with the long side. Pinch the edges and ends to seal. Put the loaves on the prepared baking sheet, seam sides down.

7. Cover lightly with plastic wrap and let rise in a warm place until doubled in volume, about 1½ hours.

8. Preheat the oven to 400°F. Bake the loaves for 30 to 40 minutes or until browned. Remove from the baking sheet and cool on a rack.

Note: Cake yeast is available at some supermarkets as well as natural foods stores.

PEAR AND HAZELNUT BREAD
· ·

Blending sweet Pear Sauce with the distinct flavor of hazelnuts and a good measure of ginger turns an ordinary loaf into a very special holiday bread redolent with the tastes of the season.

Makes 1 loaf

¾ cup packed light brown sugar
½ cup granulated sugar
½ cup (1 stick) unsalted butter, softened
2 large eggs, at room temperature
1 cup Pear Sauce, at room temperature
  (recipe follows)
2 cups all-purpose flour
1 teaspoon baking powder
½ teaspoon baking soda
½ teaspoon ground ginger
¼ teaspoon salt
Grated zest of 1 orange
½ cup finely chopped hazelnuts
¼ cup finely chopped crystallized ginger
Confectioners' sugar, crystallized ginger
  strips, and candied lemon peel, for
  garnish

1. Preheat the oven to 350°F. Butter and flour a 9 × 5 × 3-inch loaf pan. Line the bottom of the pan with waxed paper. Butter and flour the paper.
2. In the medium bowl of an electric mixer, beat the sugars and butter at medium speed until light and fluffy. Add the eggs and beat well. Reduce the speed to low and beat in the Pear Sauce.
3. In a small bowl, sift together the flour, baking powder, baking soda, ground ginger, and salt. Gradually stir the dry ingredients into the batter.

4. Stir in the orange zest, hazelnuts, and chopped ginger. Spread the batter evenly in the prepared pan.
5. Bake for 1 hour to 1 hour 5 minutes, or until a toothpick inserted in the center comes out clean. Cool the bread in the pan on a rack for 10 minutes. Remove from the pan and cool completely on a rack.
6. Dust with confectioners' sugar. Cut into squares or slices to serve. Garnish with strips of crystallized ginger and candied lemon peel.

PEAR SAUCE
· ·

Use some of this sauce in the Pear and Hazelnut Bread (see the preceding recipe), then save the leftovers to serve with roast pork. The sauce is equally delicious on its own as a last-minute dessert or snack.

Makes 3⅓ cups

5 firm pears (about 8 ounces each),
  peeled, quartered, and cored
1 lemon, peeled, quartered, and seeded
¼ to ½ cup sugar

1. In a food processor, chop the pears and lemon in several batches, using a pulsing motion. You should have about 4 cups of chopped fruit.
2. In a heavy, large saucepan, combine the chopped fruit and sugar. Bring to a boil. Lower the heat and boil gently, stirring occasionally, for about 30 minutes or until the mixture is the consistency of applesauce.
3. Puree the sauce in a food processor or blender, if desired.

SCONES
· · · · · · · · · · · ·

Bake a batch of these classic easy-to-mix scones to go with a cup of afternoon tea after a busy day of shopping or decking the house with holiday cheer.

Makes 12 to 14 scones

1¾ cups self-rising all-purpose flour
2 teaspoons sugar
1 teaspoon cream of tartar
½ teaspoon baking soda
¼ cup (½ stick) cold unsalted butter, cut
  into small pieces
⅔ cup milk

1. Preheat the oven to 450°F.
2. In a medium bowl, sift together the flour, sugar, cream of tartar, and baking soda.
3. Add the butter and blend with a pastry blender or 2 knives until the mixture resembles coarse meal.
4. Gradually add the milk, mixing with a fork just until a soft, pliable dough forms.
5. On a floured surface, knead the dough lightly with your fingertips to form a smooth dough. Gently roll out to a thickness of ½ inch. Cut the dough into rounds with a 2-inch biscuit or cookie cutter. Gather and reroll the dough scraps, cutting more scones until all the dough is used. Put the rounds on an ungreased baking sheet, spacing about 1 inch apart.
6. Bake the scones for 10 to 12 minutes or until golden brown. Serve warm with butter and fruit preserves.

CORNMEAL SAGE BISCUITS
. . . .

Do not stop with adding sage to the stuffing for the turkey. Add a pinch of dried sage to a cornmeal batter, and once baked, fold hot biscuits into a checked napkin tucked into a basket and bring the flavor of a country garden to your table.

Makes 30 small or 14 large biscuits

1¼ cups all-purpose flour
¾ cup yellow cornmeal
2 teaspoons baking powder
1¾ teaspoons finely chopped fresh sage or
  ¾ teaspon dried sage
¼ teaspoon baking soda
⅛ teaspoon freshly ground pepper
¼ cup (½ stick) cold unsalted butter, cut
  into small pieces
⅔ cup apple juice
30 extra-small or 14 small fresh
  sage leaves
1 large egg white, lightly beaten

1. Preheat the oven to 425°F.
2. In a medium bowl, combine the flour, cornmeal, baking powder, chopped sage, baking soda, and pepper. Mix together well. Add the butter and blend with a pastry blender or your fingertips until the mixture forms very small, pea-sized lumps.
3. Using a fork, gradually stir in the apple juice just until the dough is moistened and pulls away from the sides of the bowl. The dough will be sticky.
4. On a well-floured surface, pat the dough lightly with floured fingertips to a thickness of about ¾ inch.

Fold into thirds. Pat out, and fold into thirds again.
5. Gently roll out the dough to a thickness of ½ inch. Cut into rounds with a 1½- or 2-inch biscuit or cookie cutter. Gather and reroll the dough scraps, cutting more biscuits until all the dough is used. Set the biscuits on an ungreased baking sheet so that they barely touch.
6. Dip the sage leaves in the lightly beaten egg white and put one on top of each biscuit.
7. Bake the biscuits for 12 to 16 minutes, or until lightly browned. Serve warm.

MARMALADE DANISH
. . . .

Few morning treats are as easy to bake as these flaky, airy Danish pastries garnished with healthy spoonfuls of marmalade. Frozen puff pastry is easy to find in the supermarket, and you can use your favorite marmalade or make the Three-Fruit Marmalade on page 108.

Makes 18 Danish pastries

8 ounces frozen puff pastry
1 large egg, beaten
Sugar
3 to 4 tablespoons marmalade

1. Thaw the pastry according to the package directions. Preheat the oven to 375°F.
2. Cut the pastry lengthwise into 3 strips along the fold lines. Cut each strip lengthwise into six ½-inch-wide strips, making 18 strips in all.
3. Twist each pastry strip a few times. Put on ungreased baking sheets. Loosely coil each strip to form a Danish pastry with a shallow well in the center. Tuck the ends underneath.
4. Brush the pastries with the beaten egg and sprinkle with sugar. Let stand for 5 minutes. Bake for 12 minutes.
5. Remove the pastries from the oven but leave the oven on. Spoon about ½ teaspoon marmalade in the center of each pastry. Bake for 4 to 6 minutes more or until golden. Serve warm.

Marmalade's Story

As early as medieval times, British housewives made a fruit and honey concoction first called marmelo and then marmalade. At the end of the eighteenth century, a Dundee merchant named James Keillor discovered he could not sell a shipment of Seville oranges because of their bitterness. He took them home, and after a little experimenting, his wife produced the first orange marmalade. Nearly 100 years later, Oxford grocer Frank Cooper's wife made her own special marmalade to sell to undergraduates and university dons. The English breakfast tradition was launched.

BLEEDING HEART MUFFINS

How sweet on Christmas morning to break open a hot, steaming muffin and find cheerful red preserves marbled throughout. No need to spread anything on these moist sweet breads, although a pat of creamy butter is certainly a luscious addition.

Makes 30 small heart-shaped or 18 standard muffins

1¾ cups all-purpose flour
1 tablespoon baking powder
2 teaspoons granulated sugar
½ teaspoon baking soda
½ teaspoon salt
2 tablespoons packed light brown sugar
1 tablespoon grated lemon zest
¼ cup (½ stick) cold unsalted butter, cut into cubes
1 large egg
1 cup milk
6 tablespoons raspberry, strawberry, or currant preserves
2 tablespoons finely chopped fresh mint or lemon balm

1.   Preheat the oven to 400°F. Butter 30 small heart-shaped, cast-iron muffin cups.

2.   In a medium bowl, sift together the flour, baking powder, granulated sugar, baking soda, and salt. Stir in the brown sugar and zest until blended. Cut in the butter with a pastry blender or 2 knives until the mixture resembles coarse crumbs.

3.   In a small bowl, whisk the egg and milk until blended. Make a well in the center of the dry ingredients and pour the egg-milk mixture into it. Stir just to moisten. Do not overmix.

4.   Spoon about 1 tablespoon of the batter into each of the prepared muffin cups.

5.   In a cup, combine the preserves and mint and mix well. Spoon a heaping ½ teaspoon of this mixture on each muffin. Use a wooden toothpick to swirl the preserves and muffin batter together in a zigzag pattern.

6.   Bake for 15 to 16 minutes or until a toothpick inserted in the center of a muffin comes out clean.

7.   Cool in the pan for 5 minutes. Remove from the pan and cool on a rack.

Note: To make standard muffins, fill each of the 18 buttered (2½-inch) muffin cups about two thirds full and bake for 18 to 20 minutes.

> ### Sage and Rosemary
>
> *B*oth sage and rosemary have long traditions as Christmas herbs, so fragrant are their fragile leaves that perfume the house as they season the food. Both are said to thrive only in homes where the woman rules the household, and those who grow sage are meant to live long lives.

APPLE RAISIN MUFFINS

Herb-scented butter makes a delicate accompaniment to these flavorful apple muffins. The rosemary is an unexpected, delightful addition that no one will forget.

Makes 16 muffins

Rosemary Butter:

½ cup (1 stick) unsalted butter, softened
1 tablespoon chopped fresh rosemary
    leaves or ½ teaspoon dried rosemary

Apple Raisin Muffins:

2½ cups all-purpose flour
¾ cup granulated sugar
1 tablespoon baking powder
¾ cup heavy cream
½ cup vegetable oil
3 tablespoons freshly squeezed lemon juice
2 large eggs, lightly beaten
1 cup peeled, cored, and shredded
    Granny Smith or other tart apple,
    tossed with 1 tablespoon lemon juice
½ cup golden raisins
Confectioners' sugar, for garnish

To make the Rosemary Butter:

1. In a small bowl, blend the butter and rosemary with a fork.
2. Cover and let stand at room temperature until ready to serve.

To make the Apple Raisin Muffins:

1. Preheat the oven to 350°F. Butter 16 (2½-inch) muffin cups.
2. In a large bowl, sift the flour, granulated sugar, and baking powder. Make a well in the center of the dry ingredients. Add the cream, oil, lemon juice, and the beaten eggs. Mix quickly, just until the dry ingredients are moistened. Be careful not to overmix. Fold in the shredded apple mixture and raisins.
3. Fill each of the prepared muffin cups with about ¼ cup of batter so that it is three quarters full. Bake for 25 to 30 minutes or until a toothpick inserted in the center of a muffin comes out clean.
4. Cool in the pan for 5 minutes. Remove from the pan and cool on a rack.
5. Dust with confectioners' sugar. Serve with Rosemary Butter.

The Charm of Novelty

*U*pon her first taste of a penny bun, a simple yeast bread sold by every baker and muffin man in London, Queen Victoria reportedly asked, "What is that delicious little cake?"

The muffin man carried these and other small baked breads on a flat wooden tray balanced on his head as he walked the streets of London, keeping them warm with a green baize cloth. Alas, muffin men disappeared shortly before World War II. Oddly enough, what we in America call English muffins bear very little resemblance to the ones the muffin man sold.

ORANGE SOUR CREAM COFFEE CAKE WITH RASPBERRIES

Think of these miniature coffee cakes as little Christmas presents for your friends or relatives during a holiday brunch party or on Christmas morning. So sweet and warm are the handfuls of red raspberries baked in the cakes, these individual offerings surely will brighten the gloomiest winter day.

Makes 8 servings

Coffee Cake:

1 cup sugar
½ cup (1 stick) unsalted butter, softened
2 large eggs
2 cups all-purpose flour
1 teaspoon baking powder
1 teaspoon baking soda
¼ teaspoon salt
1 cup sour cream
3 tablespoons Cointreau,
    Grand Marnier, or other
    orange-flavored liqueur
1 teaspoon vanilla extract

Filling:

¼ cup granulated sugar
1 tablespoon grated orange zest
1 cup fresh raspberries, or frozen
    raspberries without syrup, thawed
    and drained
Confectioners' sugar, for garnish
    (optional)

To make the Coffee Cake:

1. Preheat the oven to 350°F. Butter and flour 8 fluted 1-cup mini-tube pans or other 1-cup mini pans.
2. In the large bowl of an electric

mixer, beat the sugar and butter at medium speed for about 5 minutes or until light and fluffy, scraping the sides of the bowl often. Add the eggs, one at a time, beating well after each addition.

3. In a medium bowl, combine the flour, baking powder, baking soda, and salt. Mix well. In a small bowl, stir together the sour cream, liqueur, and vanilla.

4. Add one third of the flour mixture and one third of the sour cream mixture to the butter mixture and beat at low speed to blend. Repeat two more times with the remaining flour and sour cream mixtures.

To make the Filling:

In a cup, stir together the granulated sugar and orange zest. Set aside.

To assemble:

1. Divide half the batter evenly among the prepared pans, using about ⅓ cup of batter for each.

2. Spoon the raspberries in a ring in the center of the batter in each pan. Sprinkle the filling over the berries. Spoon the remaining batter carefully over the berries and filling, spreading gently to cover.

3. Bake for 20 to 25 minutes or until a toothpick inserted in the center of a cake comes out clean.

4. Cool the cakes in the pans on a rack for 15 minutes. Run a thin knife carefully around the edges of the cakes to loosen them. Remove from the pans and cool completely on a rack. Dust with confectioners' sugar before serving, if desired.

VICTORIAN JAM COFFEE CAKE
· · · · · · · · · · · · · · · · · · · ·

Because fruit jams and jellies were so popular during the nineteenth century, used for the first time in imaginative culinary creations, it is not surprising that a number of different sorts of jam cakes found their way to the Victorian table. This variation on a favorite theme serves as a moist and delicious coffee cake that is especially good at teatime.

Makes 8 servings

Cardamom Crust:
¼ cup all-purpose flour
¼ cup sugar
¾ teaspoon ground cardamom or cinnamon
3 tablespoons cold unsalted butter, cut into small pieces

Coffee Cake:
1½ cups all-purpose flour
⅓ cup sugar
1 teaspoon baking powder
½ teaspoon baking soda
⅛ teaspoon salt
2 large eggs
1 cup ricotta cheese
3 tablespoons unsalted butter, melted and cooled slightly, or 3 tablespoons vegetable oil
½ cup damson plum, apricot, plum, or blueberry-lime preserves or rhubarb marmalade

To make the Cardamom Crust:

1. In a small bowl, combine the flour, sugar, and cardamom. Mix well.

2. Add the butter and blend with a pastry blender or your fingertips until the mixture resembles coarse crumbs. Set aside.

To make the Coffee Cake:

1. Preheat the oven to 375°F. Butter an 8-inch springform pan or butter and flour a deep 8-inch round cake pan.

2. In a large bowl, combine the flour, sugar, baking powder, baking soda, and salt. Mix well and set aside.

3. In a medium bowl, whisk together the eggs, ricotta cheese, and melted butter.

4. Make a well in the center of the dry ingredients. Pour in the egg mixture and stir just until combined. Do not overmix. The batter will be stiff and lumpy.

5. Spread the batter into the prepared pan. Dot the preserves or marmalade over the surface. Using a knife, gently swirl the preserves through the batter to create a rippled effect. Smooth the top and sprinkle with the crust mixture.

6. Bake for 40 to 45 minutes or until a toothpick inserted in the center of the cake comes out clean.

7. Cool the cake in the springform on a rack for 10 minutes before removing the pan sides. Or, cool the cake in the round cake pan on a rack for 1 hour. Loosen the edges of the cake with a thin knife. Carefully turn the cake out onto a rack.

8. Cut the coffee cake into wedges and serve warm or at room temperature. The cake is best served the same day it is baked.

CAKES AND DESSERTS

· ·

Quiet mornings dusted with snow, children sledding down the hill in the meadow, and church choirs practicing Christmas carols on clear afternoons are some of the best things about the season. Equally wonderful are the parties. Make yours special by preparing one or two of the desserts included on these pages. Not all are suited for fancy affairs; some are better for more intimate, informal gatherings, which are as much a part of the season as the glittering events.

· ·

GINGER POUND CAKE

· · · · · · · · · · · · · · · ·

The aromas wafting from the kitchen when you bake this simple cake will fill the house with the spirit of Christmas as few other smells do. Make several cakes so that you can give one or two away.

Makes 8 to 10 servings

Pound Cake:
3/4 cup (1 1/2 sticks) unsalted butter, softened
3 large eggs, at room temperature
1 cup sugar
1 teaspoon ground ginger
1 1/4 cups sifted cake flour

Glaze:
1/2 cup ginger currant wine (see Note)
2 tablespoons sugar
Crystallized ginger slices, for garnish

To make the Pound Cake:

1.   Preheat the oven to 325° F. But-ter and flour a 6-cup fluted black tube pan.

2.   In the medium bowl of an electric mixer, beat the butter at medium speed until very light.

3.   In a large bowl, using clean beaters, beat the eggs, sugar, and ground ginger at high speed for 6 minutes or until the sugar is dissolved and the mixture is light and fluffy. Using a wooden spoon or a rubber spatula, gently but thoroughly fold in the sifted flour.

4.   With the mixer at low speed, gradually blend in the butter. Do not mix for more than 30 seconds but continue to blend in the butter by folding gently with a wooden spoon. Spread the batter evenly in the prepared pan.

5.   Bake for 35 to 40 minutes or until the cake springs back when lightly touched. Cool the cake in the pan or on a rack for 15 minutes. Remove from the pan and cool on a rack for 30 minutes.

To make the Glaze:

1.   In a small saucepan combine the wine with the sugar. Heat over low heat, stirring, until the sugar dissolves.

2.   Put the cake on a serving platter and pierce small holes with a wooden skewer or fork on the fluted side. Slowly pour the glaze over the cake and cool completely. Wrap in plastic wrap and let the cake stand overnight to soak up the glaze.

3.   Before serving, decorate the cake with crystallized ginger.

Note: If you cannot find ginger currant wine, soak 1 tablespoon freshly grated ginger in 1/2 cup warmed cream sherry for 30 minutes. Strain the mixture before using.

HONEY CAKE WITH GINGER

A cross between a honey cake and a brownie, this confection can be served when neighbors drop by or late at night after wrapping presents.

Makes 8 servings

Honey Cake:
¾ cup honey
¾ cup milk
6 tablespoons (¾ stick) unsalted butter, melted
2½ cups all-purpose flour
¼ cup sugar
2 teaspoons baking powder
1 teaspoon ground ginger
½ teaspoon salt
½ teaspoon ground cinnamon
¼ teaspoon baking soda
¼ cup chopped crystallized ginger
2 large eggs, well beaten

Honey Topping:
1 cup heavy cream
2 tablespoons honey brandy or brandy
2 tablespoons honey

To make the Honey Cake:
1. Preheat the oven to 350° F. Butter a deep 9 × 2-inch round cake pan or an 8 × 8 × 2-inch square baking pan.
2. In a small saucepan, combine the honey and milk. Stir over medium heat until the honey is melted. Stir in the melted butter. Set aside to cool.
3. In the large bowl of an electric mixer, sift together the flour, sugar, baking powder, ground ginger, salt, cinnamon, and baking soda. Add the crystallized ginger and toss to coat.

Set aside.
4. Mix the eggs into the cooled milk mixture until blended. Add to the flour mixture and beat at medium speed just until smooth. Pour the batter into the prepared pan and lightly smooth the surface.
5. Bake for 40 to 50 minutes or until a toothpick inserted in the center comes out clean.
6. Cool the cake still in the pan on a rack for 10 minutes. Remove from the pan and cool slightly on a rack.

To make the Honey Topping:
1. Just before serving, in the medium bowl of an electric mixer, beat the cream at low speed until soft peaks form. Add the brandy and honey and beat just until blended.
2. Serve the cake warm, cut into wedges, with the Honey Topping.

CHOCOLATE CAKE WITH CHOCOLATE BUTTER ICING

This cake will satisfy any chocolate desire, and best of all, you can make it and the luscious frosting in the wink of an eye.

Makes 8 to 10 servings

Chocolate Cake:
1 cup self-rising all-purpose flour
¾ cup plus 2 tablespoons superfine sugar
½ cup unsweetened cocoa powder
1 teaspoon baking powder
¾ cup (1½ sticks) unsalted butter, softened
3 large eggs
3 tablespoons boiling water

Chocolate Butter Icing:
2 cups confectioners' sugar
½ cup (1 stick) unsalted butter, softened
2 tablespoons boiling water
1 tablespoon unsweetened cocoa powder
Walnut pieces, for decoration

To make the Chocolate Cake:
1. Preheat the oven to 350°F. Butter and flour two 8-inch round cake pans.
2. In the large bowl of an electric mixer, sift together the flour, sugar, cocoa, and baking powder. Stir until blended.
3. Add the butter, eggs, and boiling water. Beat at medium speed to blend, scraping the sides of bowl often. Increase the speed to high and beat for 5 minutes. Divide the batter evenly between the prepared pans and lightly smooth the top.
4. Bake for 25 to 28 minutes or until the edges pull away from the sides of the pans and the tops spring back when lightly touched.
5. Cool the cakes in the pans on racks for 10 minutes. Remove from pans and cool completely on racks.

To make the Chocolate Butter Icing:
1. In the large bowl of an electric mixer, combine the confectioners' sugar, butter, boiling water, and cocoa. Beat at low speed to blend. Increase the speed to medium and continue to beat until smooth.
2. Spread one of the cooled cake layers with some of the Chocolate Butter Icing. Top with the second layer. Frost the top of the cake with the remaining icing. Decorate with walnuts.

CRANBERRY SACHER TORTE

This updated version of the rich Austrian dessert bursts with plump cranberries, those bright red berries in season in November and December and so much a part of our holiday cooking. In this recipe they stud the cake, glide down its sides in a sweet glaze, and festoon the cake with lovely color.

Makes 10 to 12 servings

Chocolate Cake:
8 ounces semisweet chocolate, broken into pieces
1 cup (2 sticks) unsalted butter, softened
⅔ cup sugar
7 extra large egg yolks (½ cup)
1 cup all-purpose flour
1 cup fresh cranberries, chopped
7 extra large egg whites (1 cup)
¼ teaspoon salt

Cranberry Topping:
½ cup homemade or canned whole berry cranberry sauce
1 tablespoon rum or cranberry liqueur

Chocolate Glaze:
8 ounces semisweet chocolate, broken into pieces
⅓ cup sugar
⅓ cup water
5 tablespoons unsalted butter, cut into small pieces

Sugar-Frosted Cranberries:
Fresh whole cranberries
1 (4-ounce) carton frozen egg substitute, thawed, or 2 large eggs, lightly beaten with a tablespoon of water
Sugar
Lemon leaves, for decoration

To make the Chocolate Cake:

1. Preheat the oven to 350°F. Butter and flour a 9-inch springform pan. Line the bottom with waxed paper. Butter and flour the waxed paper.

2. In the top of a double boiler over hot, not simmering, water, melt the chocolate, stirring until smooth. Remove from the hot water and let cool slightly.

3. In the large bowl of an electric mixer, beat the butter with the sugar at medium speed until light and fluffy, scraping the sides of the bowl often.

4. Gradually beat in the egg yolks until blended. Reduce the speed to low and beat in the cooled chocolate. Gradually stir in the flour just until mixed. Fold in the chopped cranberries.

5. In another large bowl, using clean, grease-free beaters, beat the egg whites and salt at high speed until stiff but not dry. Stir one quarter of the egg whites into the chocolate batter. Gradually fold in the remaining egg whites.

6. Pour the batter into the prepared pan, gently smoothing the top. Put the pan on a baking sheet. Bake for 45 to 50 minutes or until the top is firm and springs back when lightly touched.

7. Remove the cake from the oven and cool on a rack for 10 minutes. (The cake will shrink away from the sides of the pan and settle slightly during cooling.) Carefully loosen the sides of the cake with a knife. Remove the side of the pan. Invert the cake onto a rack. Remove the pan bottom and carefully peel off the waxed paper.

Turn the cake right way up and cool completely on the rack.

To make the Cranberry Topping:

1. In a small saucepan, combine the cranberry sauce and the rum. Bring to a boil over medium heat, crushing any large pieces of cranberry with a wooden spoon.

2. Spoon the hot topping over the cooled cake and spread carefully in an even layer.

To make the Chocolate Glaze:

1. In the top of a double boiler over barely simmering water combine the chocolate, sugar, and water. Stir until the chocolate melts and the mixture is smooth. Remove from the hot water.

2. Add the butter and stir until melted. Let cool at room temperature for 30 minutes, stirring occasionally, until the glaze thickens.

3. Put the cake on a rack over a large piece of waxed paper. Slowly pour the glaze over the top of the cake, allowing some to run down the sides.

4. Let the cake stand for 1 hour at room temperature to set the glaze. If the glaze is still soft, refrigerate the cake for 1 hour before serving.

To make the Sugar-Frosted Cranberries:

1. Using a small brush, coat the cranberries with the egg substitute or egg wash. Spread the sugar in a pie plate. Roll the coated berries in the sugar.

2. Dry the cranberries on a rack or plate until the sugar hardens.

3. Decorate the cake with the frosted cranberries and the lemon leaves. The cake is best served the day it is made.

Sugar Treats from Queen Victoria's Day

The young Victoria was entranced by the magic and beauty of Christmas. Writing in her journal on Christmas Eve, 1832, the future queen reported that "after Mamma had rung a bell three times we went in. There were two large round tables on which were placed two trees hung with lights and sugar ornaments. All the presents were placed round the tree. I had one table for myself."

Later, when she married Prince Albert, the Queen embraced his devotion to the Christmas traditions of his German childhood. Many years later she wrote: "The Queen rejoices to think that the Prince and herself are the source of Christmas trees being generally adopted in this country."

LAVENDER MERINGUES

Make these pretty desserts by the trayful, as they will surely disappear during the whirl of holiday visiting. They are good served with afternoon tea or as a simple sweet after dinner.

Makes about 15 meringues

2 large eggs whites, at room
temperature
½ teaspoon cream of tartar
8 tablespoons superfine sugar
3 tablespoons fresh pesticide-free lavender
flowers or 1 tablespoon dried
lavender

1. Preheat the oven to 250°F. Line a baking sheet with parchment paper.
2. In the large bowl of an electric mixer, using clean, grease-free beaters, beat the egg whites with the cream of tartar at high speed until soft peaks form. With the mixer still at high speed, gradually add 6 tablespoons of the sugar, 1 teaspoon at a time. Beat until the mixture is shiny and holds stiff peaks.
3. Gently but thoroughly fold in the remaining 2 tablespoons sugar and the lavender flowers.
4. Pipe the meringue through a pastry bag or drop large spoonfuls onto the prepared baking sheet in about 15 (2-inch) rounds. Bake for 50 minutes. Let cool on the baking sheet for 5 minutes. Carefully remove the meringues from the parchment paper with a spatula.

MARMALADE AND CREAM LAYERS

Being able to rely on frozen puff pastry makes holiday entertaining easy and elegant. A good example of its versatility is this effortless dessert, made with layers of puff pastry spread with seductively rich whipped cream flavored with your favorite marmalade. For a change of pace, substitute raspberry or strawberry jam for the marmalade.

Makes 15 pastries

8 ounces frozen puff pastry
¾ cup heavy cream
½ cup marmalade
Confectioners' sugar, for garnish
(optional)

1. Thaw the pastry according to the package directions. Preheat the oven to 375°F.
2. Cut the pastry lengthwise into 3 strips along the fold lines. Put the strips on an ungreased baking sheet.
3. Bake for 25 minutes or until puffed and light golden brown. Cool the pastry strips on a rack.
4. In the medium bowl of an electric mixer, beat the cream at low speed until soft peaks form. Gently fold the marmalade into the whipped cream.
5. Using a thin, sharp knife, carefully cut each pastry strip horizontally into 3 layers. Put the 3 bottom layers on a serving plate. Spread ⅓ cup of the whipped cream mixture on each. Add the middle pastry layers and spread with the remaining whipped cream mixture. Top each with its remaining pastry layer. Sprinkle with confectioners' sugar, if desired.
6. Using a sharp, serrated knife, cut each filled pastry crosswise into 5 slices and serve.

Christmas Pudding

The warm, spicy, steamed pudding we know as plum pudding— even though it no longer contains plums—evolved from a dish prepared during the Middle Ages called plum pottage. The rustic dessert, so different from what we eat today, was made from beef and broth thickened with brown bread. The cook added raisins, currants, prunes, and spices such as cloves, mace and—if she was fortunate enough to have some—ginger. By Victoria's day, plum pottage had turned into a far more palatable dish called plum pudding. The prunes were replaced by extra currants and raisins and the savory ingredients were omitted altogether, save for the beef suet used as shortening. The richness of the pudding and its exotic flavors made it an obvious choice for Christmas, as did the fact that it required no fresh, seasonal ingredients. Soon it was commonly known as Christmas pudding.

MARMALADE SOUFFLÉ
. . . .

No dessert is more magical than a soufflé. Be sure the oven is nice and hot, do not linger once the ingredients are combined and ready for the oven, and remember that a soufflé, once puffed and golden, waits for no one.

Makes 8 servings

3 tablespoons unsalted butter
3 tablespoons all-purpose flour
Pinch of salt
1 cup milk, warmed
4 large egg yolks
½ cup sugar
½ cup marmalade
1 tablespoon grated orange zest
5 large egg whites, at room temperature

1. Butter and generously sugar a 2- to 2½-quart soufflé dish.
2. Melt the butter in a small saucepan over low heat. Whisk in the flour and salt. Cook, whisking constantly, for 3 minutes.
3. Slowly whisk in the warm milk. Increase the heat to medium-high and bring to a boil, whisking constantly. Remove the pan from the heat and let the mixture cool to room temperature (about 1 hour).
4. Preheat the oven to 325°F.
5. In the medium bowl of an electric mixer, beat the egg yolks with ¼ cup of the sugar at high speed for about 5 minutes or until thick and lemon-colored. Add the cooled milk mixture to the yolks and beat well. Stir in the marmalade and orange zest.

6. In a large bowl, using clean, grease-free beaters, beat the egg whites until soft peaks form. Gradually beat in the remaining ¼ cup sugar until the mixture is stiff and glossy.
7. Fold one quarter of the egg whites into the marmalade mixture. Gently fold the marmalade mixture into the remaining egg whites. Scrape the batter into the prepared soufflé dish.
8. Bake for 50 minutes to 1 hour or until the soufflé is puffed and a toothpick inserted in the center comes out clean. Serve at once.

QUEEN OF PUDDINGS
. . . .

A simple custard topped with jam and mounds of meringue becomes a regal dessert. The stock ingredients are humble bread crumbs, eggs, and milk, but the secret lies in using tangy lemon zest and fine raspberry jam to flavor the pudding.

Makes 6 servings

Pudding:
2 cups milk
1 cup fresh whole-wheat bread crumbs
2 tablespoons (¼ stick) unsalted butter,
    melted
1 tablespoon packed light brown sugar
Finely grated zest of 1 lemon
3 large egg yolks
½ cup raspberry jam

Meringue:
3 large egg whites, at room temperature
6 tablespoons superfine sugar
Whipped cream, for serving (optional)

To make the Pudding:
1. Preheat the oven to 325°F.
2. In a small saucepan, bring the milk to a boil. Pour the milk over the bread crumbs in a medium bowl. Let stand for 2 minutes.
3. Stir in the butter, brown sugar, and lemon zest.
4. In a small bowl, beat the egg yolks lightly. Stir in ½ cup of the warm milk mixture. Whisk back into the remaining milk mixture.
5. Pour the mixture into an ungreased deep 1-quart casserole. Put the casserole in a 9 × 9 × 2-inch baking pan. Pour hot water into the baking pan to a depth of 1 inch. Bake for 45 to 50 minutes or until the mixture is just set in the center.
6. Remove the pudding from the oven and let stand in the water bath. Do not turn the oven off.
7. Top the pudding with small spoonfuls of jam.

To make the Meringue:
1. In the medium bowl of an electric mixer, using clean, grease-free beaters, beat the egg whites at high speed until soft peaks form. Gradually add the sugar and continue to beat until stiff and glossy peaks form.
2. Spread the meringue over the jam layer, right to the edge of casserole. Fluff up into small peaks.
3. Bake in the same hot water bath for 20 to 25 minutes or until the meringue is light brown and set.
4. Remove from the water bath and cool on a rack. Serve warm or cold, with whipped cream if desired.

AUNTIE EM'S MARMALADE CAKE

• • • • • • • •

This old-fashioned fruit-filled cake, made with tea-soaked dried fruit and a dash or two of redolent spices, is the perfect treat to come home to after a busy round of shopping or visiting.

Makes 12 to 16 servings

Marmalade Cake:
2 cups mixed dried or candied fruit, such
    as ¾ cup chopped dried apricots, ¼
    cup chopped candied citron, and 1
    cup dried currants
1 cup hot strong brewed tea
1 cup packed light brown sugar
½ cup (1 stick) unsalted butter, softened
3 large eggs
¼ cup orange marmalade
2 cups all-purpose flour
2 teaspoons baking powder
½ teaspoons ground ginger
½ teaspoon ground nutmeg
Pinch of salt
½ cup chopped walnuts

Marzipan Topping:
1 3½-ounce roll marzipan

Marmalade Sauce:
½ cup orange marmalade
1 tablespoon freshly squeezed orange juice
Fresh orange blossoms and leaves, for
    decoration

To make the Marmalade Cake:

1.   Preheat the oven to 250°F. Butter and flour a 2-quart charlotte mold that is 7 inches in diameter and 4½ inches deep. Line the bottom with waxed paper. Butter and flour the paper.

2.   In a medium bowl, soak the fruit in the hot tea.

3.   In the large bowl of an electric mixer, beat the brown sugar and the butter at medium speed until fluffy, scraping the sides of the bowl often.

4.   Add the eggs, one at a time, beating well after each addition. Beat in the marmalade.

5.   In a medium bowl, sift together the flour, baking powder, ginger, nutmeg, and salt. Gradually beat into the batter at low speed until blended.

6.   Stir in the walnuts and mix well. Stir in the fruit/tea mixture.

7.   Pour the batter into the prepared mold. Bake for 2½ hours or until a toothpick inserted near the center comes out clean. Cool the cake still in the mold on a rack.

8.   Invert the cake onto a serving platter and carefully remove the mold and then the waxed paper.

To make the Marzipan Topping:

1.   Roll out the marzipan between 2 sheets of waxed paper into a 7-inch circle.

2.   Remove the top sheet of waxed paper. Using a sharp knife, trim the edges of the marzipan to form an even circle. Invert the marzipan circle onto the top of the cake and peel off the remaining waxed paper.

To make the Marmalade Sauce:

1.   In a small saucepan, combine the marmalade and orange juice. Cook over medium heat, stirring often, until the marmalade is melted.

2.   Pour the sauce around the base of the cake.

To serve:

Decorate the top of the cake with fresh orange blossoms and leaves. Cut into thin slices to serve.

CARAMEL PECAN PUFF TARTS

....

The chocolate-lined tartlets generously filled with nuts and sweet caramel syrup are mini pecan pies that can be enjoyed with the family or packed up and toted along as a lovely gift.

Makes about 20 tartlets or 1 tart

Pastry:
2 cups all-purpose flour
*½ cup (1 stick) cold unsalted butter, cut
    into small pieces*
¼ cup cold solid vegetable shortening
¼ teaspoon salt
3 tablespoons ice water

Caramel Pecan Filling:
*3 ounces bittersweet chocolate, broken
    into pieces*
1¾ to 2 cups pecan halves
¼ cup sugar
1 cup light corn syrup
*3 tablespoons unsalted butter, cut into
    small pieces*
3 large eggs (at room temperature)
1 teaspoon vanilla extract
Whipped cream, for decoration
Golden dragées, for decoration

To make the Pastry:

1. In a food processor, combine the flour, butter, shortening, and salt. Process until the mixture resembles coarse meal.

2. With the food processor running, gradually add ice water until the dough pulls away from the sides of bowl and forms a ball. Wrap in plastic wrap and refrigerate for at least 2 hours.

3. Roll out the dough between 2

sheets of floured waxed paper to a thickness of about ⅛ inch. With a cookie cutter, cut the dough into rounds about 4½ inches in diameter. Line about 20 (3-inch) tartlet pans with the rounds. Or, keep the dough in one piece and line a 9-inch pie plate. Put the tart pans on a baking sheet. Refrigerate the dough while making the filling.

To make the Filling:

1. In the top of a double boiler over hot, not simmering, water, melt the chocolate. Stir until smooth. Spread the melted chocolate on the bottom of the pastry shells. Refrigerate for about 20 minutes to harden the chocolate.

2. Arrange the pecans over the chocolate layers.

3. In a heavy medium-size saucepan, heat the sugar over medium-high heat, stirring constantly with a

long-handled wooden spoon until the sugar melts and turns a golden caramel color. Remove the pan from the heat. Gradually stir in the corn syrup. (The mixture will be lumpy.)

4. Return the pan to medium heat and gradually stir in the butter until melted. Continue to cook, stirring constantly, until the sugar lumps dissolve. Remove from the heat and let cool for 5 minutes.

5. Preheat the oven to 375°F.

6. In a medium bowl, whisk the eggs and vanilla until blended. Gradually whisk in the cooled caramel syrup in a slow stream until blended. Pour the mixture over the pecans in the pastry shells.

7. Bake for 18 to 20 minutes for tartlets, 40 to 45 minutes for the 9-inch tart or until the filling is set. Cool on a rack. Decorate the tartlets with whipped cream and golden dragées just before serving.

POACHED PEARS

· ·

These succulent Poached Pears form the basis for the Pear Tart (see the recipe on the following page), and they are delicious on their own or spooned over ice cream and topped with warm chocolate sauce.

Makes 2 to 3 pears

2 to 3 firm but ripe pears, peeled (about 8 ounces each)
Sweet wine such as Sauternes
Grape or apple juice (optional)
½ vanilla bean split lengthwise
2 lemons

1.   Arrange the pears in a heavy, nonreactive (enamel or stainless steel) saucepan just large enough to hold the pears lying on their sides. Add just enough wine to cover the pears. Supplement the wine with fruit juice, if desired. Add the vanilla bean and the juice of 1 lemon (see Note).

2.   Bring the wine mixture to a simmer over medium-high heat. Reduce the heat to medium low, cover, and simmer gently for 12 to 15 minutes or until the pears are tender when pierced with a fork or knife. Turn the pears in the wine several times during poaching.

3.   Remove the pears from the saucepan with a slotted spoon. Drizzle with the juice of the remaining lemon and drain well.

Note: For rosy poached pears, add 1 to 2 tablespoons grenadine to the poaching liquid.

PEAR TART

Pears are often considered a winter fruit, and few better ways exist of using the sweet, fragrant fruit than in this classic tart. The poached pears blend magnificently with the sweet pastry cream resting in the buttery crust.

Makes 6 servings

Pastry Shell:
1½ cups all-purpose flour
¼ cup sugar
Pinch of salt
10 tablespoons (1¼ sticks) cold unsalted butter, cut into small pieces
2 large eggs

Pastry Cream:
6 large egg yolks
¾ cup sugar
½ vanilla bean, split lengthwise
½ cup all-purpose flour
2 cups milk
2 to 3 tablespoons pear brandy (optional)

Apple Glaze:
½ cup apple jelly
2 teaspoons grenadine

Assembly:
3 Poached Pears (see page 132)
Praline brittle (pulverized and in pieces), for decoration
Whipped cream, for serving

To make the Pastry Shell:

1. In a food processor, put the flour, sugar, and salt. Add the butter and pulse briefly until the mixture resembles coarse crumbs.
2. Add 1 egg. Process until the dough forms a ball. If necessary, add a few drops of cold water to make the dough hold together.
3. Wrap the dough in plastic wrap and refrigerate for 1 hour.
4. Preheat the oven to 400°F. Roll out the dough between 2 pieces of floured waxed paper to a thickness of about ⅛ inch. Fit the dough into a 9-inch tart pan with a removable bottom, pressing it lightly against the pan to make sure there are no air pockets. Trim the excess dough by pressing it against the top edge. Prick the dough all over with the tines of a fork. Put the tart pan on a baking sheet.
5. Bake for about 30 minutes or until golden brown. While the pastry is baking, prick it occasionally with a fork to prevent puffing.
6. Remove the Pastry Shell from the oven. Lightly beat the remaining egg and lightly brush the egg wash over the pastry. Bake for 5 minutes more. Cool on a rack.

To make the Pastry Cream:

1. In the large bowl of an electric mixer, combine the egg yolks and the sugar. Scrape in the seeds from the vanilla bean and beat at high speed for about 5 minutes or until light and fluffy.
2. Sift the flour over the yolk mixture and fold it in.
3. Put the milk in a heavy, large saucepan and bring to a boil. With the mixer at low speed, gradually add the milk to the batter to temper it. Pour the batter back into the same saucepan and cook over medium heat, whisking constantly, until boiling.
4. Remove the pan from the heat. Whisk in the brandy, if desired. Pour the Pastry Cream into a bowl and press plastic wrap directly on the surface. Let cool to room temperature (about 1 hour). Refrigerate the cooled cream for at least 4 hours.

To make the Apple Glaze:

1. In a small saucepan, combine the apple jelly with the grenadine.
2. Melt over medium heat, stirring often. Set aside.

To assemble:

1. Evenly spread the chilled Pastry Cream into the cooled Pastry Shell.
2. Halve and core the Poached Pears. Slice each pear half into thin slices lengthwise but do not separate the slices at the base. Slide a narrow spatula under each sliced pear half, then place them on top of the Pastry Cream in a circle of slightly overlapping slices.
3. Spoon the Apple Glaze over the pears. Sprinkle with pulverized praline brittle and decorate with larger pieces of the praline brittle. Serve the tart alongside a bowl of whipped cream dotted with pieces of the brittle.

A Fruitful Harvest

An old country adage says that if you can see sun shining through the branches of the fruit trees in the orchard on Christmas morning, you will not be short of fruit come spring.

TROPICAL FRESH FRUIT TART

· · · · · · · · · · · · · · · · ·

Few desserts could be simpler or more welcome in the dead of winter than this cheerful fruit tart which utilizes many of the tropical and semitropical fruits so readily available in markets from coast to coast.

Makes 8 to 10 servings

Tart Shell:
2 cups all-purpose flour
1 cup confectioners' sugar
¼ teaspoon salt
1 cup (2 sticks) unsalted butter, cut into small pieces and softened
2 ounces semisweet chocolate, coarsely chopped

Cream Cheese Filling:
1 (8-ounce) package cream cheese, softened
6 tablespoons confectioners' sugar
2 tablespoons Cointreau, Grand Marnier, or other orange-flavored liqueur
1 cup heavy cream, whipped to soft peaks

Topping and Glaze:
Fresh fruit, such as banana, peach and/or kiwi slices, pineapple chunks, strawberry halves, raspberries, orange sections
½ cup apricot preserves, strained
2 teaspoons Cointreau, Grand Marnier, or other orange-flavored liqueur

To make the Tart Shell:
1. Butter the bottom and sides of a 9-inch tart pan with a removable bottom.
2. In a food processor, combine the flour, confectioners' sugar, and salt. Process until blended.
3. Add the butter and pulse briefly until the mixture resembles coarse meal. Continue to process until the dough pulls away from the sides of the bowl and just forms a ball. Wrap the dough in plastic wrap and refrigerate for 1 hour.
4. Preheat the oven to 350°F. On a lightly floured work surface, roll out the dough. Fit the dough into the prepared pan, pressing it lightly against the pan to make sure there are no air pockets. Trim the excess dough by pressing it against the top edge. Prick the dough all over with the tines of a fork. Put the tart pan on a baking sheet.
5. Bake for 20 to 25 minutes or until the edges are golden brown. Prick the pastry occasionally during baking to prevent puffing. Cool the shell on a rack.
6. In the top of a double boiler over hot, not simmering, water, melt the chocolate, stirring until smooth. Brush the melted chocolate on the bottom of the cooled shell. Refrigerate for about 20 minutes to harden the chocolate.

To make the Filling:
1. In the medium bowl of an electric mixer, beat the cream cheese and the confectioners' sugar at medium speed until creamy.
2. Beat in the liqueur. Gradually fold in the whipped cream with a rubber spatula or wire whisk until the mixture is smooth.
3. Spread the filling evenly over the chocolate layer in the tart shell.

To make the Topping and Glaze:
1. Drain the fruit thoroughly and arrange decoratively on top of the filling.
2. In a small bowl, combine the apricot preserves and the liqueur and mix well. Brush the mixture over the fruit.
3. Cover carefully and refrigerate the tart for at least 30 minutes to set the glaze.

RASPBERRY HAZELNUT MERINGUE

The bright red and glistening black berries peeking out from between the layers of the crisp dacquoise are a cheerful sight on a cold winter's eve. If finding fresh berries is a problem, use frozen.

Makes 12 servings

Meringue Shells:
8 large egg whites, at room temperature
Pinch of cream of tartar
Pinch of salt
2 teaspoons distilled white vinegar
2 cups sugar
2 cups ground hazelnuts or almonds
2 teaspoons hazelnut- or almond-flavored liqueur such as Frangelica or Amaretto

Fruit Cream Filling:
2 cups heavy cream
1 tablespoon sugar
1 teaspoon hazelnut- or almond-flavored liqueur such as Frangelico or Amaretto

Assembly:
½ pint fresh raspberries or frozen raspberries without syrup (about 1½ cups)
½ pint fresh blackberries or frozen blackberries without syrup thawed (about 1½ cups)
2 tablespoons confectioners' sugar
¼ cup toasted hazelnuts or sliced almonds, for decorations

To make the Meringue Shells:

1.   Preheat the oven to 325°F. Butter and flour two 8½- or 9-inch springform pans. Line the bottoms of the pans with parchment paper. Butter and flour the paper.

2.   In the large bowl of an electric mixer, using clean, grease-free beaters, beat the egg whites, cream of tartar, and salt at high speed until soft peaks form. Add the vinegar. With the mixer still at high speed, gradually add the sugar. Continue to beat at high speed for 5 to 6 minutes or until the mixture is glossy and holds stiff peaks.

3.   Gently but thoroughly fold in the ground nuts and the liqueur. Divide the meringue between the prepared pans, spreading gently so that each is slightly higher at the edges and sinks a little in the center.

4.   Bake for 1¼ hours or until the meringue is pale brown and pulls away from edge of the pan. Remove the meringue layers. The meringue will fall in the center as it cools.

5.   Run a knife around the edges of the pans to loosen the meringues. Remove the sides of the pans. Using a thin spatula, loosen the meringues from the parchment paper. Remove the paper.

To make the Fruit Cream Filling:

In the large bowl of an electric mixer, beat the cream at low speed until soft peaks form. Beat in the sugar and liqueur just until blended.

To assemble:

1.   Put 1 meringue shell right side up on serving plate. Reserve ½ cup of the Fruit Cream Filling, for decoration.

2.   Fill the meringue with half the remaining filling and all the berries. Spoon the remaining filling over the fruit.

3.   Set the second meringue layer upside down over the filled layer. Sift confectioners' sugar on top. Decorate with the reserved Fruit Cream Filling and the toasted nuts. Refrigerate for at least 1 hour or up to 6 hours to allow the meringue to soften. Cut with a serrated knife to serve.

TRADITIONAL FAVORITES

Christmas is the most beloved of holidays, when tradition is king and everyone recalls sweet memories of childhood. Now more than any other time, we rely on what has gone before to give structure and meaning to the season.

What follows are some of the best recipes of a classic nineteenth-century English Christmas. Some have been updated, tailored for the modern cook who, despite restricted time, wants to create the most memorable of holidays for family and friends.

JOY'S EGGNOG

Few holiday parties seem complete without a punch bowl full of the custardy, potent drink, generously sprinkled with nutmeg floating on its surface like fairy dust. In old England, a milky drink called hot posset was served to ward off winter's chill, accomplished as much by the temperature of the brew as by the handy doses of ale or sherry stirred into it. Once in America, the drink was refined, enriched, and spiked with readily available alcohol such as bourbon, rum, and hard cider. Ours is a luscious combination of eggs, cream, milk, brandy, and rum thickened with billowing egg whites just before serving.

Makes 20 to 25 punch cup servings

6 large eggs, separated
¾ cup plus 4 tablespoons sugar
1½ cups brandy
1½ cups rum
3 cups whole milk
3 cups heavy cream
Freshly grated nutmeg, for garnish

1. The day before serving, in the medium bowl of an electric mixer, beat the egg yolks with ¾ cup of the sugar at high speed for about 8 minutes until thick and lemon-colored.
2. Beat in ½ cup of the brandy and ½ cup of the rum.
3. Pour the mixture into a nonreactive (enamel or stainless steel) container. Cover and refrigerate overnight to develop the flavors. Put the egg whites in a tightly covered container and store in the refrigerator.
4. Chill a 6-quart punch bowl, a large mixing bowl, and beaters. About 30 minutes before serving, remove the egg whites from the refrigerator and allow them to come to room temperature.
5. Just before serving, pour the egg yolk mixture into the chilled punch bowl. Whisk in the remaining 1 cup brandy and 1 cup rum, and the milk.
6. Put the cream in the chilled bowl and beat with the chilled beaters until it begins to thicken. Gradually add 2 tablespoons of sugar and beat until soft peaks form. Slide the whipped cream into the punch bowl.
7. In a medium bowl, using clean, grease-free beaters, beat the egg whites at high speed until soft billows form. Gradually add the remaining 2 tablespoons of sugar and continue to

PUNCH MARQUIS

Here is a sweet, easy, dramatically flaming punch to serve on frosty nights in front of a roaring fire when no one is in much of a hurry to go home. Pour a cup and let everyone bask in the warmth of your hospitality.

Makes 8 to 10 punch cup servings

1 (750-ml) bottle Sauternes
1 cup sugar
2 whole cloves
Zest of 1 lemon, cut into large strips
1¼ cups brandy
Thin orange or lemon slices, for garnish

1. In a medium saucepan, combine the Sauternes with the sugar. Add the cloves and lemon zest. Warm over medium heat until the mixture simmers, stirring until the sugar dissolves.
2. While the wine is heating, warm the brandy in a shallow saucepan. Do not let it boil.
3. Remove the lemon zest and cloves from the wine with a slotted spoon. Pour the hot wine into a heat-proof serving bowl.
4. Pour all except ¼ cup of the warmed brandy into the serving bowl. Remove the saucepan from the heat. Carefully ignite the remaining brandy with a long kitchen match and pour it into the punch.
5. When the flames subside, ladle the punch into glasses or cups, garnished with thin slices of orange or lemon.

beat until soft peaks form when the beaters are lifted.

8. Using a rubber spatula, scoop the beaten egg whites into the punch bowl. With a very large whisk or spoon, gently fold the whipped cream and egg whites into the eggnog base until incorporated but still very fluffy and light.

9. Sprinkle the eggnog with grated nutmeg. Ladle into cups and serve immediately.

QUICK FRUIT CAKE

Traditional fruit cakes are dense, heavy confections left to macerate in tumbler after tumbler of rum or brandy, poured over the cake as it ages during the weeks before Christmas. Our recipe requires no such fussing, and the result is far lighter than the dark cakes of days gone by. The traditional marzipan topping adds a sweetness not found with any other garnish. However, you may leave it off and choose instead to frost the cake with a simple white icing.

Makes 12 to 16 servings

Cake:
10 tablespoons (1¼ sticks) unsalted
  butter, cut into small pieces
¾ cup milk
6 tablespoons light corn syrup
2 tablespoons molasses
1 cup walnut pieces
1 cup dried currants (4 ounces)
¾ cup pitted dates, chopped (4 ounces)
¾ cup golden raisins (4 ounces)
¾ cup dark seedless raisins (4 ounces)
¼ cup mixed chopped candied peel
  (2 ounces)
1¾ cups all-purpose flour
2 teaspoons pumpkin pie spice
½ teaspoon baking soda
2 large eggs
2 tablespoons brandy

Marzipan Topping:
Confectioners' sugar
1 (7-ounce) roll marzipan

Apricot jam or honey

To make the Cake:
1. Preheat the oven to 300°F. Butter an 8 × 8 × 2-inch baking pan. Line the bottom and sides with a double layer of waxed paper. Butter the paper.
2. In a heavy, large saucepan, combine the butter, milk, corn syrup, and molasses. Add the walnuts, currants, dates, raisins, and candied peel. Stir over medium-low heat until the butter is melted.
3. Increase the heat to medium and bring the mixture to a simmer. Simmer for 5 minutes, stirring occasionally to prevent sticking. Remove from the heat and let cool for 10 minutes.
4. In a large bowl, sift the flour, pumpkin pie spice, and baking soda. Add the cooled fruit mixture and the eggs, and whisk until blended.
5. Scrape the batter into the prepared pan. Bake for 1½ hours or until a toothpick inserted in the center comes out clean.
6. Cool the cake in the pan on a rack for 5 minutes. Remove the cake from the pan and cool completely on a rack. Trim a thin slice from the top of the cake to make it flat and even. Prick the top of the cake all over with a skewer. Sprinkle the brandy over the top of the cake.

To make the Marzipan Topping:
Lightly dust a work surface with confectioners' sugar. It helps to dust the rolling pin with confectioners' sugar, too, to prevent sticking. Roll out the marzipan to an 8-inch square.

To assemble:
1. Invert the cake onto a serving plate. Brush the uncut top surface with apricot jam or honey. Press the marzipan layer on top of the cake and dust with confectioners' sugar.
2. If desired, heat 2 or 3 metal skewers until red hot. Press into the marzipan to make a caramelized lattice pattern, repeating until the pattern is complete.

Gifts of Currants

During the last century, dried fruits were considered quite a luxury. Although Christmas giving between business acquaintances was not nearly as prevalent as it is today, nineteenth-century tradesmen presented treasured customers with sacks of currants during the Christmas season. No doubt, the sweet, succulent fruits were very welcome during the cold, damp, dark days of a London December— and probably ended up in the Christmas pudding.